# SHORT CUTS

INTRODUCTIONS TO FILM STUDIES

T0324245

# FILM PROGRAMMING

## CURATING FOR CINEMAS, FESTIVALS, ARCHIVES

## PETER BOSMA

**WALLFLOWER**

LONDON and NEW YORK

A Wallflower Press Book
Published by
Columbia University Press
Publishers Since 1893
New York • Chichester, West Sussex
cup.columbia.edu

Wallflower Press® is a registered trademark of Columbia University Press

Cataloging-in-Publication Data is available from the Library of Congress

ISBN 978-0-231-17459-6 (pbk.)
ISBN 978-0-231-85082-7 (e-book)

Book and cover design: Rob Bowden Design
Cover image: *The Long Day Closes* (1992). © Film Four International / BFI

# CONTENTS

## ACKNOWLEDGEMENTS

In this book I have tried to assemble the knowledge gathered over several decades of learning and practising. I had the privilege to attend a series of indispensable courses in film history and film analysis. I am indebted to the teachings of Prof. André Vandenbunder, Hans Saaltink, Eric de Kuyper, and film director Harry Kümmel. The department of film studies at the University of Utrecht, directed by Prof. Frank Kessler, continues to be a source of inspiration, especially through its invitation of many prominent guest lecturers such as film historian Robert C. Allen. Happily enough, founding professor William Urricchio is still a regular visitor. A continuous force of inspiration and instruction are the lectures of Prof. David Bordwell at the Summer Film colleges in Flanders, as are his flow of writings in books and blog posts. Kristin Thompson is also an exemplary researcher and writer, to whom I am likewise indebted.

In addition, I have had the rare chance to observe instructive best practices of curating films, initially during my extended internship at the International Film Festival Rotterdam in the 1980s. The late founder and first director of the festival, Hubert Bals (1937–88), was a charismatic and passionate advocate of authentic cinema; he influenced greatly a lot of movie buffs of my generation. My cinematic horizon was further broadened by my participation as a volunteer at an independent cinema in Utrecht, owned by film director Jos Stelling. At that time he also founded the Netherlands Film Festival. My focus continued to be on non-commercial film exhibition, building up experience at film theatres in Gouda, Heerlen and Maastricht, and finally working as co-programmer for two decades at cinema LantarenVenster in Rotterdam. For the first ten years I assisted Leo

Hannewijk, a man with a continuous flow of wonderful ideas and the talent to realise nearly all of them. More recently, the 2012 and 2013 editions of DigiTraining Plus organized by Media Salles were indispensable to get a thorough update of the most recent developments in the professional field.

This book is the result of a course in analysing film programming that I taught for several years at the University of Utrecht. Many thanks to the groups of Bachelor students who endured my lectures and a dazzling stream of notes. This book is the kind of volume I would have been delighted to read a long time ago as a young student of cinema culture; I hope that many members of the current generation of students have the same feeling and that this book meets their expectation.

There is a lot of information in this book and many references to recommended books. With such a broad range of subjects it is difficult to keep a right balance of density and clarity, avoiding both extremes of being superficial and getting too detailed. My editor Yoram Allon at Wallflower Press and his team, as well as dedicated external readers and reviewers, kept me on track and corrected many errors. The result is now in your hands. You might consider purchasing the book in order to study it, or possibly to react to or expand upon it. I hope you do all of these things.

There are many people who deserve a salute and a thank you, but they all know already that I am much indebted to them. Therefore I would like to dedicate this book to new and subsequent generations of cinephiles and curators.

Peter Bosma
Rotterdam, Spring 2015

# INTRODUCTION

This book offers an exploration of essential issues concerning the phenomenon of selecting films and presenting them on a big screen, to a paying audience, whether at a film theatre, film festival or film archive. This overview is aimed at several kinds of readers: those who want to become film curators themselves; those who are researching the phenomenon of film curating; and those who are critical cinema visitors who want to investigate the story behind the process of selection of the film supply for their local film theatre, film festival or film archive. In addition, I hope that film professionals involved in this process are challenged by the content of this book to discuss their trade and craft. The recent digitisation of distribution and exhibition has changed the conditions of the industry; in this book I reflect cautiously on the inevitable consequences.

The central activity in the domain of film exhibition is known as 'programming films', or 'curating films'. Maybe the latter denotation sounds a little bit presumptuous for some members of this group of professionals, but in my view it is about time to acknowledge that all of the various film programmers worldwide are 'custodians of cinema culture'. This means that their screenings should offer a varied supply of worthwhile film productions. This also means that they should present a diverse selection of the most recent releases, and simultaneously keep the varied and complex past of cinema alive through screenings of all sorts of film heritage. An additional challenge is to attract the largest possible audience for every cinema programme offered.

In order to attract an audience, it is wise to start to see things from the perspective of the film viewer. A film never exists on its own. There are a lot of other films and there is a wide context. For a film curator it is therefore important to reflect upon the question of which films members of the audience are likely to have seen and in what order, because every film you see changes the way you watch other films. An awareness of this sharpens the decisions of the film curator about the choice and the order of films in his or her programme. This issue could be expanded into a general research question in reception studies. Audience responses to the same film can be different, depending on a person's age and the general circumstances of the local film culture, and responses will also change throughout time, on both an individual and a collective level (see, among others, Allen 2011).

Considering the influence of the order in which films are viewed can also be an interesting personal reflection for the curator, who might ask him or herself which films he or she saw, in what order, and what consequences can be distinguished. The answer will underline the importance of advised film curatorship. A person's individual chronology of film viewings and their story of film experiences are set in the context of many other personal stories and also the general historical and social context. The way someone experiences classical films especially will be dominated by their expectations, based on their personal experiences and the way these films are shown.

This can be illustrated by an example: did you have the chance to see *Metropolis* (Fritz Lang, 1927) anywhere? Almost every film set in a futuristic urban environment with a dark gothic atmosphere seems to be inspired by *Metropolis*; look for instance at images of *Batman* (Tim Burton, 1989). This silent film classic is about a mad scientist who constructs in his lab an evil woman-robot (or 'female cyborg'). This theme reminds us of the *Terminator* and *RoboCop* cycles, among others. The art direction of the apocalyptic vision of an intimidating big city (or futuristic urban dreamscape) reminds us of films like *Blade Runner* (Ridley Scott, 1982), *The Fifth Element* (Luc Besson, 1997) and *Minority Report* (Steven Spielberg, 2002). In which order did you see these films? What influence has this had on your viewing experience? Perhaps you also saw the Japanese animation film *Metoroporisu* (Rintaro, 2001), which was influenced by the classic *Metropolis*, or maybe you started with the music video for 'Radio Gaga' (Queen) or 'Express Yourself' (Madonna), which also directly refer to *Metropolis*. Maybe you had the chance to watch other German silent fiction films from the 1920s, like *Nosferatu, eine Symphonie des Grauens* (*Nosferatu, a Symphony of Terror*, F. W. Murnau, 1922). It is fascinating to reflect upon the question of how these films fit in your personal viewing timeline. In what way did it influence your opinion of *Metropolis*?

Chapter one of this volume sketches the definitions of the fundamental concepts that are explored throughout the book and reflects upon the options for doing research on historical and contemporary practices of film curating. Chapter two explores the phenomenon of cinephilia from the perspective of the film curator. Chapter three then offers a concise characterisation of the network of intermediaries: film distribution, the issue of copyright and the phenomenon of film criticism. Chapter four discusses the programme and audience of a film theatre. Chapter five elaborates on the varied characteristics of the international film festival circuit. Chapter six investigates the fundamental tasks of film archives and discusses the definition of film heritage. After these enquiries into the main avenues of exhbition, chapter seven offers two case studies of curating a film programme; and chapter eight consists of a tentative justification of film art and an exploration of the essence of cinema, with reference to film's future prospects in the twenty-first century.

Students are advised to start with chapter one and proceed with chapter three. General film enthusiasts could start with chapter two and continue with chapter eight. Researchers are welcome to test the scope of chapters four, five and six. Film professionals are invited to start with chapter seven... But naturally all are free to read at their own discretion.

The purpose of the book is to provoke solid thought and analysis on the act of film curating. It is a slippery subject because it lacks rigid or institutionalised standards. This book thus aims to give film curating some footing and to observe this activity as:

- a creative act, expressing an artistic identity
- a management challenge, mapping costs and expenses, return on investment, opportunities to realise growth of the company or festival, the focus is on entrepreneurship
- a social phenomenon of artistic value, that needs analysis and explanation

- a craft or skill that can be learned by professional training, with a focus on smooth logistics, optimising practical processes of specific project management

These four strands are connected and all of them are equally important. They can be placed in a quadrant like this:

|  | practice | theory |
|---|---|---|
| artistic | creative act | social phenomenon |
| business | management challenge | craft |

# 1    REFLECTION

In our lifetime we all collect special experiences of screenings in cinemas and we cherish the memories of them. There is a whole industry at work to make this possible. This book focuses on the end of the decision chain. The purpose of this book is to analyse the activity of selecting films and scheduling them purposefully for screening to an audience, whether at a film theatre, film festival or film archive. This activity could be described as 'curating film' or 'film programming'. What do these terms mean, precisely? This calls for clarification. The next step is to investigate the practice of contemporary film curating as a worthwhile subject of research. Historical research on curating film programmes is also explored, and a list of relevant general research questions is offered. Then, the phenomenon of presenting films professionally is discussed from an institutional perspective. This approach serves as a tool for mapping the artistic choices of the film curator and analysing them in a systematic way.

## 1.1 Definitions and Demarcations

The phenomenon of film presentation has a varied context in the digital age. We may focus on films shown on the big screen, but films are everywhere: outdoors in the public space there are many urban screens, and in the personal environment one can consume films at any time. The term 'film' refers here to the phenomenon of a public screening of a film for a paying and attentive audience in a film theatre, at a film festival, in a film archive or elsewhere. These options need some specification. A 'film theatre' is a venue for film screenings through the year. Subdivisions could be made on the basis of identity (art-house cinema or commercial venue; first-run theatre offering premieres or repertory cinema offering revivals) and size (the number of seats and the number of screening rooms). A 'film festival' is a temporary series of film screenings and side programmes, presented as a unified event. A subdivision of film festivals could be made on the basis of the geographical scope, thematic range and overall purpose of the festival. A 'film archive' is an institution dedicated to conserving, preserving and restoring film heritage. For a definition of 'film heritage', see section 6.1.

Here the term 'film curator' is used to indicate the person who compiles a film programme. The term 'curator' is associated predominantly with art galleries and museums, but could be applied to the field of film exhibition as well. The term 'film programmer' is frequently used in the international film industry, but could prove a bit confusing because in the information technology industry the designation of 'programmer' refers to someone who undertakes computer programming. Naturally, it is possible to disregard possible misunderstandings and continue to use the term 'film programmer', focusing on the scheduling of screenings, and many do so, but I choose here to use the label 'film curator' as it connotes a more sophisticated level of cinematic knowledge than simply 'programming' specific screenings.

The process of making artistic choices is a common phenomenon in the cultural field. In the music industry a DJ selects music for dance events, club nights or radio programmes. In the television industry a scheduler selects the content of a broadcast for a station or channel. In the world of fine arts a curator selects content for an art biennale or museum, or presentations of collections. There is also the more recent phenomenon of 'content curation' performed by both digital information professionals and amateurs, selecting and filtering content of social media on the Internet. The term 'format' is mostly used to indicate the style or arrangement of a programme idea for (commercial) television; this is comparable to a magazine format. A cinema programme can also have a format, with recurring items and a recognisable line-up.

A film curator is a person who selects films for public screenings, using various criteria, to be held either in a film theatre, at a festival, in a film archive or elsewhere. In each case, the curator has a dual responsibility: to compose an interesting programme and attract a large enough and, hopefully, loyal audience. In other words, the curator's goal is to obtain a measure of critical acclaim and provide the highest possible customer satisfaction. A film curator organises inspiring programmes and events, and brings together films and people, enabling exchanges and encounters. His or her core task is to create *added value* in cultural terms, set in a context of negotiating financial conditions, coordinating a smooth workflow, and overcoming repressions and restrictions.

This general definition of a film curator could be compared with the more specific definition given by four film heritage experts, Paolo Cherchi Usai, David Francis, Alexander Horwath and Michael Loebenstein, who limit themselves to the world of film archives and formulate a more restricted definition of 'film curatorship': 'The art of interpreting the aesthetics, history, and technology of cinema through the selective collection, preservation, and documentation of films and their exhibition in archival presentations' (Cherchi Usai *et al.* 2008: 231).

This book, then, is about the story behind the organisation of curated content in the domain of cinema: someone prepares a set of film screenings and hopes to attract a significant audience to attend and enjoy this programme. From an economic perspective, a film curator is just a small part of a larger whole. Seen from a business point of view, a film curator is not considered to be the decisive decision-maker. Therefore, the focus here will be on the characteristics of artistic choices but also on the context in which these choices are made and mediated. The curatorial practice consists of a daily struggle with deadlines. Firstly on an artistic level: choosing which films are to be programmed next week, next month, next season. Secondly on a financial level: how this will be paid for. There is also the urgent need to address marketing challenges: how to attract an audience and gain critical attention. The task of a film curator is, furthermore, to act as the moderator of a relevant conversation and instigator of audience participation and engagement. To organise the screening of a film programme is certainly a high-pressure task.

A film curator also has to retain his or her passion and curiosity, despite the pressure and routine of consecutive deadlines. The challenge is to keep an open mind, to continue to explore recent publications and magazines and to visit various film festivals. A film curator is supposed to be cautiously receptive to associations, intuitions and promptings, in combination with having the discipline to do lots of research in order to cut down the long list of possible choices and to compile the final selection in the best possible way. Every film curator has to perform a delicate balancing act in emphasising traditions of film art on the one hand and deconstructions of these traditions on the other. The central challenge is to learn from experiences and evaluations of logistics, but also to be able to explore new approaches and to be open to new ideas and new ways to present both film heritage and film releases.

There are a wide range of causes and effects of successful curating, which could be formalised in conditional critical success factors (CSFs) and evaluative key performance indicators (KPIs). The creation of curating concepts needs to be connected to a strategy of fundraising and marketing efforts. To support the analysis of best practices of entrepreneurship applied to curatorial practice there exists a wide body of guidelines and methods, taken from business theory and specialisations such as project management and marketing strategy. Using tools like systematic checklists and audits, it is possible to perform insightful benchmarking. The focus in this book, however, is strictly on discussing issues concerning the creation of a valuable film programme. But the context of business considerations remains in the background.

The core function of a film curator could be described as being a 'gatekeeper' or a 'cultural intermediary'. Both terms are derived from sociological research into the cultural industries, mass communication and journalism (see, for example, Shoemaker and Vos 2009). A gatekeeper's main function lies in selecting which cultural events the spectators get to see or hear. Taking its meaning most literally, a gatekeeper functions as a strict doorman who decides who and what is getting access to an audience and the media. But a gatekeeper is never one person acting alone. The decision chain in the film world consists of an interdependent network of producers, sales agents, distributors, curators and critics. This complex pattern of collective decision-making is based on, for example, assessing the potential profitability of proposed projects and searching for new content for existing successful formats. In contrast, a cultural intermediary acts as a matchmaker or go-between, who focuses on discovering new talents and new approaches, and introducing them to a new audience at the best possible venue.

## 1.2 Mapping the Artistic Choices of the Film Curator

This introductory chapter focuses on analysing and discussing the position and function of a film curator. Before practical issues are discussed in the next chapters, here I will sketch a framework to organise the background information in a systematic way. There is a scientific approach labelled institutional analysis that aims at gaining insight into the mechanisms of the presentation and circulation of culture in general. The phenomenon of artistic choice, furthermore, is highly relevant in the domain of the humanities, because this is the key to understanding the actual supply of culture, and also the historical developments in this area. Who decides which cultural expressions are to be seen and heard regularly, which of them are being safeguarded in accessible archives, and which of them are surfacing in school textbooks, and ranked as generally accepted cultural heritage?

There is a fierce existential competition, both for sheer presence and attention and for appreciation and remembrance. A film curator should have an opinion about the essentials of cinema history and the fundamentals of their contemporary film practice. Stefanie Schulte-Strathaus (2004) discusses the practice of 'showing different films differently', in relation to the film archive. Her central argument is that films are products of a specific place and time and are watched by a viewer with a specific background of knowledge and experience. In the ideal situation a film curator has a clear and innovative artistic vision that adds value to the chosen films. Three actions are necessary: creating a strong programme, embedding that programme in a relevant context, and making the programme attractive for a sufficiently large crowd.

Each film curator is part of an 'economy of ideas', based on a particular exchange value: salaries are paid for constructing a brilliant programme concept. The audience is part of an 'economy of experience': the cinema ticket is paid for in exchange for a special and lasting viewing experience. The twenty-first century is characterised by a transition from the era of ownership to the 'Age of Access', as Jeremy Rifkin (2000) labelled it in his book of the same name.

Film curators are the masters of their cinema venue, but they have to relate themselves to a complex network of connections between several actors and aspects. The position of a film curator is characterised by a strong dependence on suppliers. To begin with, there are film producers with a wide range of reputations, from unknown new talents to respectable established names. Next come the intermediaries, most prominently the sales agents and distributors who are a part of the infrastructure of the film industry, but also the network of governmental institutions that provide an essential context of cultural policy and support. On the reception side is the powerful force of the audience and the influence of peers and independent experts. One of the first distinctions to make in this ramified network is at the level of the mobility of films: what route do they take; where are they screened? The international chain of film distribution provides a constant supply of films that need to be processed, filtered and promoted. This flow of official releases can be supplemented by film curators with relevant exclusive programming. Therefore it is necessary to consider also the mobility of film curators: what research they do, what trips they undertake, what discoveries they make and what kind of constraints and restrictions they encounter.

The position of film curators has changed due to developments in the networks of both the production and the consumption of films. The film curator of today is to be regarded as a node of connections in a network, functioning in a period of transition. Scientific research into the curatorial practice is a challenging exercise in posing the right questions, to discover patterns which transcend daily routines.

How can we map relevant developments, evaluate them and possibly explain them? It all starts with a systematic inventory of the whole spectrum of collaborations, conflicts and constraints. Here follows an initial brainstorm of possible specifications in this area, translated into a provisional list of issues to be addressed: Which patterns are to be distinguished in film circulation? What are the criteria for the selection of films and choice of distribution channels? Which opinions and ambitions are noticeable in the network of intermediaries? Which forces filter the availability and preservation of films? Which characteristics mark the collective viewing habits, appreciation and remembrance? Which target groups are addressed and reached? These questions are part of a current debate in a wide range of scientific institutional research in the humanities focused on the circulation of culture, in such disciplines as media studies (television, radio, the Internet), art history (galleries, auction houses, museums), literary studies (publishers, magazines, bookshops, libraries), musicology (the music industry, concert halls, orchestras), theatre studies (festivals, companies, playhouses and other stages) and even religious studies (forms of liturgy, selection of sacred texts). In the humanities a holistic approach prevails, meaning that the object, in our case the film programme, is analysed in its context of political-legal, economic, social-cultural and technological aspects. In many textbooks this spectrum of external influential forces is summarised by the abbreviation PEST.

There is still no substantial and comprehensive institutional theory of film production, distribution and exhibition. The American film theorist Noël Carroll made an initial attempt in an article originally published in 1979, in which he takes the aesthetics of the American philosopher George Dickie as a starting point (reprinted in Carroll 1996). Happily enough, there are a few outstanding case studies published in the domain of institutional research of film circulation, such as that of Kristin Thompson (2008), who offers an analysis of the international marketing campaign and release of the *Lord of the Rings* trilogy (Peter Jackson, 2001, 2002, 2003). This is a fascinating story, from both a business and an artistic perspective.

*Film curating: film production*

First of all we need filmmakers, people who are creative and have the stamina to develop their ideas and realise outstanding films. They are confronted by fierce competition in terms of contemporary talent and a huge heritage in the form of the output of their predecessors. What is the story behind the scenes? Institutional art theory is a subdiscipline of art sociology, and this specific perspective offers a useful framework for developing systematic reflection on the creation of films. American sociologist Howard Becker made a lasting contribution with his book *Art Worlds* (1982). His central concept is that creating art is a collective activity: it is the result of the cooperation and also obstruction of many. Even the most autonomous and individual artist still needs other people to make his or her art possible: people offering different forms of support such as education, supply of materials, channels of distribution and critical discourse. Behind each work of art Becker observes a layer of background stories about necessary conditions of assistance, support, collaboration and cooperation. This could be supplemented by also identifying a range of conflicts, constraints, rivalry and competition. Creating art involves a more or less coherent connection between many interacting parties and forces. This complex configuration is called an 'art world', a term which was first used by art

11

critic Arthur C. Danto in 1964. Becker offers an inspiring reflection on the production, distribution and consumption of art. His concept of art worlds could easily be applied to 'film worlds'. Films could be considered as nodes in several networks, among others the influence of government cultural policies and market forces, and the exchange of viewing experiences in the (inter)national public domain and on a personal level. The mapping of the dynamic relations between a configuration of nodes in a network and the flow of interaction between them could also be approached through the method of the 'Actor Network Theory' (ANT). However, for an elaboration of this perspective there is need for more space than this introduction permits (but see, among others, Latour 2005).

What are the necessary and sufficient conditions to be an artist? According to Becker, it is useless to try to define art using a compilation of specific intrinsic features. Traditional aesthetics formulates various criteria of realism, expressionism and poetics of form and style. Becker considers these value concepts as just one of the many social factors in the dynamics of an art world. His focus is on the story behind the scenes, with special attention paid to the analysis and understanding of reputations and conventions. He addresses the position of the artist in general, distinguishing three main categories. The majority of film artists are best described using his label 'integrated professionals'. In the film world there are just a small amount of outsiders ('folk artists', 'naive artists'). The most interesting category is what Becker calls 'mavericks', the unruly and self-willed artists. Orson Welles is often considered a maverick, due to his unconventional use of existing institutionalised practices and his career on the edges of the industry. This understanding could be the justification for a film curator to devote a film programme to his films. There are a lot of other directors who ignore conventions, both in the domain of film style and in the context of movie business, for example David Lynch, Jean-Luc Godard and Peter Greenaway. A film curator could choose to focus on selecting an overview of films from individual mavericks, or put them in a context of equivalent talents, or contrast them to relevant counterparts.

*Film curating: film reception*

Film exhibition forms another challenging starting point for reflection, the focus this time being on the details of the audience. Who is sitting in the screening room, under which conditions, resulting in which reactions? Film reception is a dynamic phenomenon. The same film could result in different reactions (physical, emotional, cognitive), expressed individually or collectively. Reactions could also change due to different circumstances. For example, it could matter a lot if you watch a film in an empty auditorium or a packed house, on your own or with a group of friends. Watching a film is an open process of participation in the creation of value, which evokes individual responses and shared experiences and memories. Art-house cinemas are filled by immobile spectators, sitting in darkness, with no distractions, resulting in a variable degree of identification with the space and time of the film narration, of entering the world displayed on screen.

The French film theorist Roger Odin (2000) uses the term 'semio-pragmatics' to indicate a double process of communication. On the one side you have the process of production of meaning by filmmakers of all sorts; on the other you have the process of construction of meaning by spectators. Members of the film audience have different competences and are affected by different settings. Odin distinguishes several possible ways of seeing a film. One possibility is the autonomous aesthetic view, which focuses on ascribing an aesthetic value to the film, recognising beauty and denominating quality. Another is the informed view, which recognises the signature of the 'auteur', locating the position of the film in the institutional context of the art world. By choosing a way of seeing a film, the spectator appropriates that film. The setting and circumstances of a cinema screening, meanwhile, could be analysed using the concept of 'cinema dispositif' (originally a French term, also translated as 'cinema apparatus'). It distinguishes four interacting aspects of film reception. Firstly, the possibilities of technology: the parameters of projectors, editing, and the camera. Secondly, the circumstances of the film projection: the positioning of the spectator, the codes of behaviour in a cinema. Thirdly, the film text: suggestion of time and space, construction of narrative, and options for symbolic meanings. And fourthly, the psychological processes of the cinema spectator: codes and conventions of perception, mental schemata or frames of mind.

The contemporary practice of film exhibition and reception is partly determined by historical developments, and research into former film cultures is therefore relevant. This calls for an elaboration of a historical research perspective.

## 1.3 Historical Research into Film Curating

On first sight, the fundamental setup of film exhibition seems to have not changed much throughout time. Basically, there has always been a row of chairs and a screen and a flow of projected moving images. And usually there is a room full of people eager to see what will be shown on the screen. The details of the programme and the context of the screening room have changed significantly, however. Historical research indicates that there are many differences to be noted in economic, technological and legal circumstances. This dynamic process is worth describing in detail and analysing. In what way has film exhibition been dealt with in the past? In what way did people react at these screenings?

Film curators should know their roots. Curating film started in 1895, famously with the first public screening of the Lumière brothers in Paris. This timespan of roughly 120 years offers film historians a wide field of cultural practice to investigate. Gregory Waller (2002), among others, offers a series of case studies situated in the United States over several decades. This research perspective leads to more questions about distinctive patterns in the context of cinema exhibition. How were films distributed? What kind of films were shown in cinemas? What kind of audience was sitting in the screening room? Who reacted in which ways? What were the characteristics of the critical discourse? The phenomenon of cinema has made a transition from being a new medium in 1895, through a period of a few decades in which movies were a mass entertainment medium only, to an end point as one of many cultural leisure options. This transition has had consequences for how screenings have been organised. The dispositifs of cinema can be analysed in a historical way, sorted into three kinds of screenings: in cinemas, at film festivals and in film archives.

European art-house cinemas for example have organised themselves in an international network called CICAE, established in 1955. In 1992 the European Commission started a support regulation for the European cinema infrastructure, the network of 'Europa Cinemas' as part of the MEDIA programme, together with the information and promotion service of Media Salles. What influence on the programming of cinemas did these various institutional networks have? This question is too general to be answered simply. But it could be made more specific by comparing, for example, the programme of a non-commercial cinema in 2014 with a non-commercial cinema in the same town in the 1970s, or with a film club in the 1920s. David Bordwell (2012) gives a historical overview of the film exhibition culture in the US, with a focus on his hometown, Wisconsin, and an assessment of the situation in 2012, dominated by the transition to digital projection. The American film magazine *Cineaste* organises regular round tables of exhibitors, distributors, archivists and film festival curators, to discuss the current issues in their business (see, for example, Rapfogel 2010, a critical symposium about repertory film programming; see also chapter four in this volume). The first international film festivals were held in the 1940s and 1950s, and their number expanded considerably in the 1970s and 1980s. Nowadays there is a vast international film festival circuit, consisting of a multitude of festivals worldwide. It is possible to attend a film festival each day of the year, and still you would have to select your destination out of an incredibly wide choice of options. Historical research into film festivals could focus on questions such as: Which aesthetic discussions were held in the founding years, in what way are these issues still topical, and in which way has the artistic format of successful international film festivals developed or altered? (Further discussion of this topic can be found in chapter five.) The first film archives originate from the 1930s, and have expanded steadily through the years. The international network consists of around 160 national film archives worldwide. Which developments are to be discerned in this institutional field of film preservation and presentation of film heritage? This question is further elaborated on in chapter six.

In academic film studies there has been a paradigm shift to what is know as 'revisionist' or 'new' film historiography. Robert C. Allen and Douglas Gomery provide the first clear overview of the new approach to film historiography in their groundbreaking handbook *Film History: Theory and Practice* (1985). James Chapman (2013) gives a more recent overview of developments in this field of research, also called 'the history of film history'. The revisionist film historians started with a systematic self-reflection on doing film historical research. They wanted to broaden their scope, to chart, for example, which artistic developments outside the canon of classic masterpieces are to be distinguished, which transitions in the economic and political context are recognisable, and which causes and explanations could be given for this, based upon which primary and secondary sources. The history of cinema is analysed as part of a larger media history, but at the same time the subject of research is made more specific and precise.

This shift in attention in academia resonated in the world of film archiving too, made visible among other ways through thoroughly documented restorations of formerly ignored films. For a film curator the shift in film historiography has resulted in a vast increase in repertoire.

One of the representatives of this new research focus is the American film historian Robert C. Allen. He advocates research into the history of local film exhibition, with a focus on which films were shown in which way, and making a connection to the general conditions of film culture and social conventions:

> The local places of moviegoing ... need to be re-presented not as autonomous, neutral, static places that contain audiences and movies, and that then can be 'compared' to other such places somewhere else, but as internally heterogeneous nodal points in a social, economic, and cultural cartography of cinema: intersections of overlapping trajectories, networks, trails and pathways, whose identities are constructed through the connections and collisions that occur there. (2006: 24)

Allen's call for new work fits within an increasing interest in focusing on local film exhibition, both by academic researchers and by a lot of amateur historians. The result is a huge supply of case studies of local film venues. The research of local film exhibition has become a dynamic field of research, characterised by several international cooperations like the HOMER Project (History of Moviegoing, Exhibition and Reception) and various international scholars gathering regularly at conferences such as the Society for Cinema and Media Studies (SCMS), the European Network for Cinema and Media Studies (NECS) and Domitor, the international society for the study of early cinema.

### 1.4 Questions Regarding Film Curating

The process of curating film in the past and present can be described as a complex phenomenon of selecting and presenting a cinema programme. Research into this process starts with designing a systematic approach. This is difficult to do, because there is continuous change in the film world. It is a dynamic network consisting of several interacting levels and nodes, each with differentiated intentions and motivations. Film producers are the sources of content for cinema programmes; film distributors serve as an intermediary in the supply line; film exhibitors have direct contact with customers. How can we map all the mutual power structures of agency, measure influence and dependence, and define the shifting lines of competition and alliances, constraints and cooperation, opposite and common interests, idealism and opportunism? Furthermore, all levels of the film world function within a complex context. What is the precise definition of these surrounding forces, and which consequences exactly can be noted?

To get a grip on these very general questions, I propose to start by discussing three fundamental choices about the possible focus in one's research. Firstly, an analysis can be diachronic or synchronic. A diachronic analysis concerns itself with the evolution and change over time of curating film, while a synchronic analysis of a cinema programme takes it as a working system at a particular point in time without concern for how it has developed to its present state. Secondly, there is a choice between a focus on either the artistic features or the economic reality of the cinema programme. Thirdly, research methods can be quantitative or qualitative. Quantitative research aims to measure and weigh indicators of performance. It is all about numbers and amounts. Quantitative research could answer questions concerning which films were released in a certain period of time, in which theatres, in how many screenings and attracting how many visitors. In contrast, qualitative research aims to gain an understanding of underlying reasons and motivations, to provide insights into the setting of a phenomenon, to uncover prevalent trends in thoughts and opinions. Qualitative research could be focused for instance on mapping the motivations of cinema visitors, their experience of screenings and their memories.

The next step in formulating relevant research questions is to make a clear distinction between the three levels of doing research: inventory, analysis and explanation. In the inventory phase researchers determine their definitions and assemble relevant primary and secondary data. This data search can be done through several possible methods, such as archival research, desk research, interviews and surveys. Then these data must be evaluated in an analysis, and lastly the results need to be explained, for example by determining relations of cause and effect. In explanatory critical research, the analysis and assessment might be focused on the mechanism of, for example, suppression or empowerment. However, charting influencing factors is very difficult to do, because the reality of curating does not fit into a neat laboratory setup of controlled experiments. A common research strategy therefore is to choose a 'best practice' case study approach. The selection of an excellent project or person could be done qualitatively on the basis of personal statements of experts, or quantitatively on the basis of indicators (benchmarking). The aim of this research strategy is to determine in a measurable way the source of success in this specific case.

Whatever the researcher's choices are, it is necessary that the research is valid and relevant. Even for professional researchers, these requirements are difficult to reach. Analysing curatorship should be considered institutional research, a subdivision of empirical research based on direct or indirect observation of experiences and phenomena. The first step is to collect evidence-based data. This could be facts and figures or opinions and value judgements. The next step is to formulate possible explanations or to define underlying patterns, based on clear logical deductions or inductions. The most difficult results to obtain are irrefutable conclusions such as substantiated causal relations, or valid predictions. An important phase of the empirical methodology, therefore, is the process of verification and falsification. It is not possible to write a manual that would guarantee impeccable research, but there exist several useful guidebooks, such as Saunders *et al.* (2009).

I will finish with a rough indication of two possible pitfalls in doing research. One of the most common mistakes is to get lost in the starting phase of making an inventory of the situation. It is indeed fun to collect a lot of data about cinema programmes and screenings, but there is a danger that what is produced will be just a loose account of examples, lists and anecdotes. The ultimate goal of research is to analyse the importance of the data, and to find out which general tendencies can be discerned. In order to do so, researcher needs to ask sharp questions. Hopefully this chapter provides an inspiration for this.

Another mistake for the researcher is to focus too much on the context of the cinema programme and to attribute too much significance to a lot of economic and social facts. In this way it is easy to forget the core object of enquiry: the wonderful films that are shown, in memorable screenings.

Researchers need to keep in mind which films ignited their passions, and where their fascination for cinema started. Maybe this first chapter has not entirely avoided this pitfall, but in the next chapters there is more room for manifestations of my own admiration for film art.

## 2    CINEPHILIA AS A CURATORIAL ELEMENT

Film curators should be cinephiles themselves, and their cinema programmes should preferably contain films by directors who are cinephiles, while the audience should also ideally contain a significant percentage of cinephiles. But what is the exact meaning of cinephilia, and how can this be taken as a connecting theme for curating a film programme?

### 2.1 Defining Cinephilia

The literal translation of 'cinephilia' is 'loving cinema'. This phenomenon is extremely ambiguous; it could be approached from various different perspectives and angles. Basically, a cinephile sees a lot of films. The key question is, what underlying motivation for this peculiar behaviour can be distinguished? In formulating an answer, we could mark a general dichotomy between intrinsic artistic value and instrumental social value. On the one hand, if you consider cinema to be an autonomous art, the ultimate aim in watching films is to have an aesthetic experience. On the other, if you consider cinema as a community art, a means to realise a socially involved ideal or express a committed argument, you are watching films in an activist frame. Both approaches have qualities and neither exists as a pure extreme. Below I outline five identifiers of a passion for cinema, each of which could be considered within the dichotomy of intrinsic and instrumental value.

First and foremost, cinephilia could be seen as a general way of forming a shared identity, a group of like-minded people. This shared identity is confirmed at international film festivals, in specialised film theatres and in some corners of the Internet. From this perspective, cinephilia is part of the construction of local and global clans. More specifically, cinephilia could be labelled an individual character trait of persons in the cinema audience, watching films frequently and in a devoted manner, which could be regarded as a peculiar way of spending free time. The documentary film *Cinemania* (2002), for example, shows us a few 'movie buffs' in New York, perfect representatives of this typically metropolitan cinephiliac subculture. Some people perceive this subculture as eccentric and weird; for others the portrayal is extremely recognisable, depending on one's level of cinephilia. Anyway, it is possible to raise many meaningful questions around this particular way of watching films, such as which films are seen and admired by cinephiles, in which circumstances, and which traces of the viewing experience are left in speech, writing and memory. The rise of videotape and especially DVD has changed the pattern of film consumption, sharply dividing it into two different modes of reception: on the one hand the hypnotic immersive way of watching films collectively with many others in a screening room, and on the other the more distanced, personalised individual viewing experience. The Internet has opened up possibilities for anyone to share their thoughts and experiences with anybody willing to read their user comments or blogs; therefore the amount of testimonies to cinephilia is staggering.

Secondly, cinephilia could also be a source of inspiration for film directors in many different ways. The awakening of cinephilia could be part of a memory of a youth, as in *The Long Day Closes* (Terence Davies, 1992), a portrait of a boy living in Liverpool in the 1950s. Or film directors can express their nostalgic longing for a film culture of the past, as Bernardo Bertolucci did in *The Dreamers* (2003), a fictional portrayal of young cinephiles in Paris in the 1960s. Italian director Davide Ferrario situated his poetic film about a love triangle, *Dopo Mezzanotte* (*After Midnight*, 2004), in the National Film Museum of Torino. This fascinating building is the domain of dreams and stories, a counterforce to the more brutal reality the protagonists experience outdoors. There is a large body of films about filmmaking, offering a carefully constructed peek behind the scenes, often bursting with cinephilia. There are many examples of this, but *La Nuit Américaine*

21

(*Day for Night*, François Truffaut, 1973) is arguably the most prominent, because the director profiled himself in both his films and his life as the ultimate gentle and devoted cinephile. There are many more examples to be found if we search for cinephiliac film productions. The French film *The Artist* (Michel Hazanavicius, 2011) offers a stunning homage to the era of silent films. A film like *The Purple Rose of Cairo* (Woody Allen, 1985) is a humorous salute to the Hollywood studio films of the 1930s. Another referential film is *The Good German* (Steven Soderbergh, 2006), which contains stylistic elements and narrative tropes taken from films like *A Foreign Affair* (Billy Wilder, 1948), *The Third Man* (Carol Reed, 1949) and *The Man Between* (Carol Reed, 1953). We can continue to mention many fascinating examples, such as *Far from Heaven* (Todd Haynes, 2002), a tribute to the melodramas of Douglas Sirk, especially *All That Heaven Allows* (1955). And many films from the Coen brothers can be considered masterful and passionate pastiches of several different film genres: *The Man Who Wasn't There* (2001), for instance, is an homage to film noir. Film directors can also express their admiration for a specific film of one of their predecessors, as Gus Van Sant did with his 1998 remake of Hitchcock's *Psycho* (1960). Director Martin Scorsese is rightfully considered as an authority in the field of film heritage. In 1997 he made the documentary *A Personal Journey with Martin Scorsese through American Movies*, a testimony to his admiration for Hollywood films, especially from the 1930s and 1940s. A few years later he also promoted the appreciation of classics of Italian cinema, taking his memories as a young cinephile as a starting point in his compilation of video lectures *My Voyage to Italy* (1999). Film curator and documentary maker Mark Cousins made *The Story of Film: An Odyssey* (2011), an impressive 15-hour overview of past and present film art worldwide (see Rosenbaum 2013). In Europe, two cinephiliac celebrations led to international nostalgic compilation films: *Lumière et Compagnie (Lumière and Company*, 1995), produced to celebrate the Centennial of Cinema, and *Chacun son cinéma (To Each His Own Cinema*, 2007), produced to mark the sixtieth anniversary of the Cannes Film Festival. To finish this stretch of name dropping, the domain of found footage offers other possibilities to process cinephiliac fascinations into new films, as was done for example in *Phoenix Tapes* (Matthias Müller and Christopher Girardet, 1999), in which fragments of several Hitchcock films are reworked into an artistic response (section 7.2 offers a brief introduction to the phenomenon of found footage, considered from the perspective of curating cinema exhibitions). Several experimental film directors and media artists have expressed their cinephilia through reflection and experiment by exploring the boundaries of cinema in new approaches to film form, or in expanding their canvas into installations. Artist Tacita Dean is a prominent representative of this approach, as her installation *FILM* (2011) in the huge Tate Modern Turbine Hall proved (see, on this, among others, Eakin 2011 and Smith 2012).

Thirdly, cinephilia could be described as a marketing tool within the film trade, because it can be an explicit guideline for intermediary forces in the industry. Some distribution companies and DVD labels position themselves as sensitive to cinephiliac values in their decisions as to which films they release. A film curator needs a receptive audience to realise the full potential of a film programme. The practical consequences of this fact are described in chapter four, but here we focus on the characterisation of a specific part of the cinema audience, the segment of 'movie buffs' or 'cinephiles'. From a marketing perspective this group is not a large target audience any more, but it is still important to address it, as it contains opinion leaders and critical enthusiasts. An international website like mubi.com is a significant portal to reach this target group.

Fourthly, cinephilia can also be seen as a critical method, a foundation for evaluation (see also section 3.3 for an elaboration on film criticism). Taking the personal cinephiliac experience as a starting point for a review is an internationally accepted phenomenon within film criticism. In particular, the French cinephilia of the 1950s and 1960s became famous as a practice of watching films and responding to them in a polemic way, arguing about taste and the importance of specific films and filmmakers. This Parisian subculture and its key figures stood in the broader context of society and institutional forces, in the form of the eccentric programming of the Cinémathèque Française and the editorial policy of film magazines such as *Cahiers du Cinéma* and *Positif*. Some critics became film directors themselves, grouped together as the 'French New Wave': François Truffaut, Jean-Luc Godard, Eric Rohmer and Jacques Rivette, among others. In international terms, there are more film directors who excel in critical writing, such as Peter Bogdanovich, Wim Wenders and Alex Cox. To be sure, you do not need to be a professional film critic or film director to be able to give a cinephiliac evaluation of films. Every devoted cinephile can develop a personal interpretation and emotional response.

One popular strategy is the construction of mutual cross-references and resemblances, which might remain invisible to outsiders but offer inspiration for fellow cinephiles. The personal memory mingles two films and two concepts of cinematic imagination. An observation of comparable themes and different variations is blended into a unique viewing experience. The result is the construction of fresh views on intertextual relations. To clarify this, here are some examples of the possibilities for the cinephiliac game of free associations, matches and clashes between selected films. The train ride of Johnny Depp in *Dead Man* (Jim Jarmusch, 1995) reminds me of the train ride of Lilian Gish in *The Wind* (Victor Sjöström, 1928). Both scenes are striking metaphors for travelling to another civilisation; both are fascinating opening scenes of a 'dissonant western'. The frantic search for a stolen bicycle in *Ladri di Biciclette* (*Bicycle Thieves*, Vittorio De Sica, 1948) can be compared with the frantic search for a stolen gun in *Nora iru* (*Stray Dog*, Akira Kurosawa, 1949). Both films are situated in a devastated city marked by the aftermath of World War II, in a guilt-ridden country. And one last example: Jeanne Moreau is a very gifted actress, able to convey several moods and emotions in one sequence, just by silent actions or by walking around. In *La Notte* (Michelangelo Antonioni, 1961), for instance, she walks aimlessly through the suburbs of Milan, watching her surroundings without reaction. She has returned to the neighbourhood of her youth, pausing in a difficult phase of her marriage and contemplating the inevitable death of a friend who is terminally ill. Her face reflects a spectre of despair, melancholy, grief and withheld anger. Her walks make the film memorable. *Ascenseur pour l'échafaud* (*Lift to the Gallows*, Louis Malle, 1958) is the most famous proof of this. Two years later Jeanne Moreau acted in a lesser-known film, *Moderato Cantabile* (1960), directed by Peter Brook and based on the book by Marguerite Duras. There is a plot of murder and love, but what I remember most clearly is her walk around a small harbour town in France, bringing her small son to his piano lessons.

Fifthly, the above-mentioned exercise of associative cinephilia can be taken as a source for curating film and assembling surprising weekly programmes or double bills. This most alluring perspective is further explored below. But first we need to elaborate on cinephilia as a strategy for historiographic research, because besides being a lively practice, all of the above-mentioned perspectives also have a rich past. Cinephilia is both a relevant subject and a strategy for historiographic research, a fruitful mode of reflecting on cinema. This historiographic approach can be a valuable inspiration for film curators.

## 2.2 Cinephilia as a Strategy for Historiographic Research

Christian Keathley (2006) sees the contemporary cinephile as a kind of *flâneur*. He argues for doing research into this way of film watching, which is at the same time aloof and intense, distracted and engaged. The essential insight Keathley offers is his argument about the importance of writing a film history of cinephilia to document and research the 'cinephiliac moment'. He would like to return to the astonishment of the early film viewers. It is said that they did not care so much about the main action, but were amazed by the movement of tree leaves in the background. Keathley also argues for research from the perspective of cinephilia, to write a 'cinephiliac history'. In his view, most of the academic film histories lack the signs of passion for their object of study. Keathley pleads for a new approach to film research, but he avoids a polemical tone. He cheerfully proposes to indulge in an 'irrational' film historiography (2006: 130). In his last chapter he gives an example of this approach in a line-up of five case studies presented as 'cinephiliac anecdotes'. His strategy is to choose an arbitrary fragment, a detail of a film which is not generally noted as important. He avoids the spectacular scenes, which are duly highlighted by the narrative; instead he explores a particular way of watching, motivated by cinephilia. Keathley discusses five of his favourite films: *The Searchers* (John Ford, 1956), *Bonnie and Clyde* (Arthur Penn, 1967), *Shadow of a Doubt* (Alfred Hitchcock, 1943), *Laura* (Otto Preminger, 1944) and *Rebel Without a Cause* (Nicholas Ray, 1955). He offers an inspiring overview of cinephiliac research and practice, focusing on the developments in France in the twentieth century.

A valuable addition to Keathley's study can be found in Marijke De Valck and Malte Hagener's collection (2005). This compilation of academic essays gives a good overview of the international debate around cinephilia, supplemented with a varied series of case studies where the authors try to translate a personal cinephiliac experience into a general research question. Charles Leary, for example, describes his visit to the film archive of Hong Kong, where he saw the economic value of a film catalogue. Big media concerns were earning a lot of money with old movies. The issue of quality was neglected in the process: most of the time the films were put on DVD in bad shape. Wanda Strauven recalls a special moment of zapping through the channels of a TV set in an American hotel room. Despite her jet lag she was fascinated by some flashes of images, which proved to be the classic movie *Les Carabiniers* (Jean-Luc Godard, 1963). This raises the question how it is possible that one can recognise quality in an instant, and how it is possible that an old movie is more eye-catching than a wide choice of contemporary broadcasting. One more example: Gerwin van der Pol looks back on his cinephiliac viewing experience in 1986, watching *A Zed and Two Noughts* (Peter Greenaway, 1985) on its Dutch premiere. His perception was influenced by another viewing experience, of the then recent Dutch film *Witte Waan* (*White Madness*, Adriaan Ditvoorst, 1984). He tries to figure out the phenomenon of what he calls 'the cinephile game', the origin of a special sort of pleasure: the cinephile develops with his or her informed gaze a personal interpretation, based on cross-references and resemblances at the level of theme and style which remain unnoticed to others but allow fellow cinephiles to put forward fresh views on intertextual relations, as described earlier. These few examples call for a continuation and expansion in a series of other case studies, possibly in the form of audiovisual essays.

### 2.3 Cinephilia as a Curatorial Strategy

This personal approach to film historiographic research is very inspiring for film curators, because the case studies mentioned above incite the irrepressible urge to augment this parade of fondly remembered film moments with a few more examples and put them in an appropriate context.

For instance, I am time and again impressed by the beautiful opening scene of *Fat City* (John Huston, 1972), which has a remarkably simple set-up: a man (played by Stacy Keach) wakes in his hotel room and walks to the boxing gym, accompanied by a song by Kris Kristofferson. That is all, but it is mesmerising. *Fat City* is a peculiar specimen of the subgenre of boxing films, but also belongs to the special category of American auteur cinema of the 1970s, the 'cinema of loneliness', as described by Robert Kolker in his well-known book (2011). The 1970s is also the era of 'New Hollywood', as described by Thomas Elsaesser, Alexander Horwath and Noel King (2004), amongst others. *Fat City* could be programmed with a film noir boxing film such as *Body and Soul* (Robert Rossen, 1947) but also with films filled with existential doubts and traumas, such as *Midnight Cowboy* (John Schlesinger, 1969) and *Mean Streets* (Martin Scorsese, 1973).

Another cinephiliac moment occurred for me at the end of the French film *Le Boucher* (*The Butcher*, Claude Chabrol, 1970). For many critics the most striking scene is when a class of school children have their outdoor lunch during a hike in the hills. From above a ledge, a few dark red drops of blood fall suddenly on the snow-white sandwich of one of the kids. This indeed gives an effectively shocking effect, but not a lasting impression. The story is located in a small rural village in France, plagued by mysterious murders of women. In the small community suspicion arises, centred on the local butcher, who indeed has a traumatic past. He is attracted to the new school teacher (played by Stéphane Audran), but she is not responsive to his shy advances. She has strong doubts about him and also enough internal disturbances of her own. At the end of the movie she sits outside at dusk lit up by the headlights of her car, torn by painful feelings of guilt and doubt. This description of the end scene does not qualify as a plot spoiler, because the film is so open-ended that the distinction between perpetrators and victims remains unclear. Such masterful depiction of complex and ambiguous characters can also be found in the films of, for example, the Iranian director Asghar Farhadi, for instance in *Jodaeiye Nader az Simin* (*A Separation*, 2011) and *Le Passé* (*The Past*, 2013).

Cinephilia can be an overarching strategy of curating a film festival. Kenneth Turan's book on film festivals (2002) contains a series of journalistic impressions of three festivals with aesthetic agendas: Pordenone, Lone Pine and Telluride. Marijke De Valck (2007) describes the International Film Festival Rotterdam as an example of a festival with a boldly cinephiliac programme, influenced by a global cinephiliac culture and attended by a mixture of local and international audiences. Approaches to curating film festivals are further described in chapter five.

A good example of cinephiliac curating is offered by experimental filmmaker Guy Maddin and his wife Kim Morgan, who were invited as guest curators to the 2014 Telluride Film Festival. They chose six films, starting with *M* (Joseph Losey, 1951), a Hollywood remake of the famous classic film directed by Fritz Lang in Germany in 1931. The festival catalogue describes their motivation:

Finally! A restored copy of Joseph Losey's under-seen, under-discussed, and that overused but, in this case, apt term, underrated remake of Fritz Lang's classic. It should make those tiresome souls who spit on all remakes realize it can be done with brilliantly effective deviations. David Wayne, in a quietly, powerfully weird performance, terrorizes children in a 1950s Los Angeles made evocative and seedily beautiful by cinematographer Ernest Laszlo. From the very first shot to the stunning hunt in the Bradbury Building, Losey and Laszlo submerge you in a sick and lonely old world, whirling together and propelling us towards the story's powerful mob hysteria.

The phenomenon of cinephilia itself could be taken as a connecting theme for curating a film programme. There are many options to choose from here. Italian cinema, for instance, offers several intriguing portraits of cinephiles of the celluloid era. Take for example Maddalena, the character played by Anna Magnani in *Bellisima* (Luchino Visconti, 1951). Every night she watches the films that are screened in the open air at the inner court of her tenement in Rome. Her fierce longing to belong to the dream world of cinema motivates her to take her little daughter to a screen test in the film studios of Cinecittà, only to be deceived by her own blind ambition. After much turmoil, she returns to her more safe and satisfying position as cinema spectator. Another example is to be found in *Prima della Rivoluzione* (*Before the Revolution*, Bernardo Bertolucci, 1964), a story about a young man, Agostino, a passionate cinephile (and most likely also a symbolic representation of the director). The protagonist is characterised by a mix of irony and sincerity, a character with tragic romantic dimensions. The same could be said of the passionate cinephile Nicola in *C'eravamo tanto amati* (*We All Love Each Other So Much*, Ettore Scola, 1974). We see him in his early years as an emotionally responsive spectator, attending screenings of Italian neorealist films in small film clubs. Three decades later he finds his knowledge exploited by the entertainment industry of television: he participates in a silly film quiz that ends with ignorance and indifference. Sadder and wiser, he returns to his isolation and his fond memories. Of course, director Giuseppe Tornatore made the ultimate feel-good movie, *Cinema Paradiso* (1988), featuring a projectionist who initiates a young boy into the wonderful world of cinema. Taiwanese director Tsai Ming-liang offered a more morose reverie of a disappearing cinema in Taipei in his film *Goodbye, Dragon Inn* (2003), of which Jean Ma (2010) provides an insightful analysis.

Naturally, it is also possible to choose regular, straightforward screenings of masterpieces of film art. This enables the audience to celebrate and enjoy cinema classics in their full glory, to savour the highest levels of cinematographic accomplishment realised by excellent teams. Options include magnificent films like *Touch of Evil* (Orson Welles, 1958), *Tengoku to jigoku* (*High and Low*, Akira Kurosawa, 1963), *Andrey Rublyov* (*Andrei Rublev*, Andrei Tarkovsky, 1966) and *Sayat Nova* (*The Colour of Pomegranates*, Sergei Paradjanov, 1968). These are indeed totally different films, the only similarity being that it is time and again a treat to see them presented in a perfect setting on the big screen.

*2.4 Remapping Cinephilia*

In the twentieth century a cinephile could be defined as a person who visited cinemas inordinately often and therefore developed a wide-ranging taste. The traditional cinephile lived in a local community of soulmates and immersed him or herself unrestrictedly in the experience of watching a lot of films on the big screen. In the twenty-first century, 'the age of digital reproduction', the possibility of breaching the linear elapsing of time has increased. This fundamental change calls for remapping the concept of cinephilia, as is demonstrated in the publication of a steady flow of essays, compiled in thematic editions of journals (among others *Senses of Cinema* [see Erickson 2004], *Framework* [see Buchsbaum & Gorfinkel 2009] and *Cinema Journal* [see De Valck 2010]) and book publications (for example Martin & Rosenbaum 2003 and De Valck & Hagener 2005). Barbara Klinger (2001) offers a pioneering study of the contemporary cinephile, who is eager and able to build a private collection of film heritage. The research questions she raises are still valid today:

> How, for example, is a sense of membership in the world of film connoisseurs cultivated? What kind of aesthetics dominates film collecting and how do they renegotiate established values for media objects? How have the discourses of new media technologies penetrated contemporary home film culture and affected the

way films are seen and discussed? What, finally, are the relations between the enterprise of collecting, consumerism and the private sphere? (2001: 139)

As mentioned earlier, the focus in this book is on film exhibition on the big screen, and it therefore ignores the technological and economic developments in the markets of home cinema: DVD, pay TV and all sorts of online cinema (video on demand (VoD) distribution, streaming video websites). There is a big difference between the two modes of film presentation. Film exhibition in a theatre is a service industry, operating by scheduled appointments. The core activity is providing a collective viewing experience. Home cinema on the other hand is a fundamentally different mode of distribution and watching films. It is to be considered as a consumer-goods business, ideally offering an individualised film experience, through personalised media with a high degree of platform mobility for the users. However, in practice the accessibility and mobility of data is still often problematic, due to a lack of universal technological specifications, legal differences between territories and different business approaches by providers. We need another label for this market, because 'home cinema' is not appropriate any more: many people watch films on mobile devices while they travel in trains, planes and automobiles. This large dislocated audience, which watches films individually or in small groups of family members or friends, is an important part of film culture – maybe not yet in an economic sense, due to widespread unauthorised viewings and the slow start of VoD revenues, but certainly in terms of attention. New techniques are making online access to film heritage and new film releases increasingly easy, by means of satellite channels and websites. We are witnessing the convergence of television and the Internet ('smart television') and an increase in the 'second screen' experience. In addition there is a growing number of possibilities for storage of film files in digital clouds and digital lockers. The availability of home cinema is determined by a fundamentally different set of gatekeepers. The composition of one's personal menu of home cinema becomes more and more a question of filtering the supply automatically by means of computer algorithms. From a pessimistic point of view, this means that the attention of the film consumer is determined by a self-affirming taste schedule. The question raised is whether it is desirable to be locked up in your own preferences. The answer is a matter for discussion. One author who addresses this subject, for instance, is Eli Pariser (2011), who identifies the dangers of an algorithmic world, labelled as 'The You Loop'.

The American economist Jeremy Rifkin noted as early as 2000 that we are living in 'The Age of Access'. The new economic structure is characterised by the label 'experience economy' or 'network economy'. The central concept is not personal property any more, but the accessibility of experiences. This may sound obvious, because today we indeed see the possession of videotapes or DVDs replaced by access to streaming video on a leased smartphone. In this new constellation the providers compete fiercely for the attention of the consumer, because consumers pay dearly for their connection to essential networks. Added value is now measured in experiences, not property. This means that imagination is the core of the experience economy and intellectual property forms the means of capital. Instead of a distinction between the haves and the have-nots, the new social distinction will be between 'connected' and 'disconnected'. Rifkin sketches a gloomy picture, warning us that if we are not careful our whole life will be one big lease contract. If you can pay enough, all your troubles will be taken care of, from cradle to grave. He sees the contours of a privatised welfare state, based on the law of the richest. American film researcher Chuck Tryon argues that the new technological possibilities of the on-demand culture have wider implications in the domain of privacy. He warns us that we are being registered in a detailed way:

> Contemporary media platforms actively solicit an individualized, fragmented, and empowered media consumer, one who has greater control over when, where, and how she watches movies and television shows. However, this offer of liberation from the viewing schedule is often accompanied by increased surveillance, giving studios, streaming video services, and social media companies more precise information for their efforts to market directly to those individualized viewers. (2013: 14)

*Questions, questions...*

We have moved into the era of participatory culture. The film viewer has increasingly become an active participant in the circulation of films. The

31

threshold for filmmaking has become lower and lower, because it has become relatively easy to contribute to the supply of audiovisual material. The threshold for film distribution has also become easier to pass, because the Internet offers unprecedented facilities for establishing international interaction. The public can exchange content and their experiences with each other, in direct dialogue with peers or inspired by popular opinion unveiled by algorithmic logic. Digital visual culture is dominated by a staggering accessibility and a dizzying supply of television channels, a huge variety of computer games and the existence of many video databases, cluttered with submitted audiovisual material. The most famous example is the website YouTube, which was launched in 2005. It is therefore possible to realise a lot of curating ideas offered in this book at home. Some DVD labels encourage this option through a vast supply of tantalising DVD box sets, or by offering well-curated series like 'Masters of Cinema'.

This freedom of choice and possibility for interaction sounds very democratic, because it strengthens the autonomy of the individual consumer and is an example of an independent self-managing market based on freedom of information flows. But what role remains in this situation for quality control by the curator, the eccentric expert? How do we keep the unlimited options on offer on the Internet navigable; in what way do we bring some reasoned clarity to this endless ocean of communication and information capabilities? Countless voices are able to speak in increasingly high numbers, but who listens? How can all these cultural offerings be assessed in a meaningful way? Will the great common denominator not determine the dominant tastes and reduce the supply of films to a limited selection of top hits and bestsellers? Or will the domain of art cinema fragment into numerous niche markets, autonomous small-scale international subcultures, idiosyncratic access codes and demarcations of highly particular canons? Is there a future for traditional film exhibition, based on scheduled shows and projections on the big screen? The next chapter explores some of the relevant and essential conditions of traditional film exhibition, namely film distribution, copyright issues and value judgements in film criticism.

# 3 THE NETWORK OF INTERMEDIARIES

A film curator is part of a network of intermediaries. This chapter selects three front lines in this constellation. Film distribution companies are the main suppliers for a curator, therefore it is necessary to know how film distribution functions. The main obstruction for a free choice of films is formed by constraints of screening rights, therefore the issue of copyright needs to be evaluated. Each film programme and each film release flourishes with a reasoned response from film critics, therefore this domain also deserves further exploration.

## 3.1 A Concise Exploration of Film Distribution

This section describes international developments in the traffic of cinema, on the level of both business deals and informal distribution. Film distribution traditionally forms the connection between film production and film exhibition. In the digital age however, the traditional distribution companies do not offer exclusive access to films anymore. For a long time now cinemas have not been the only possible location for watching movies. Release windows are vanishing and will soon disappear totally, and the same content will be available everywhere at the same time. Therefore, it will become more important for film curators to present a diverse and unique programme, to create an experience that adds value for their customers. In order to be able to do so, we need to explore alternative business models for a profitable circulation of film. Regarding the adjustment of the traditional distribution deal, the most basic questions are: who pays which part of the costs of investments and maintenance, and who gets which part of the profit? As a consequence of the recent digitisation of the film exhibition, a new structure of financial deals and alliances is needed between exhibition firms, distribution companies, integrators, film producers and sales agents. A financially strong company is essential for a flourishing market, because a strong market leader enhances the quality of the infrastructure and the solvency of the industry. In addition, a niche market aiming at minority target groups is necessary to guarantee a dynamic supply, because it serves like a Research and Development division in a traditional business environment.

It is possible to grade the quality of a national film culture according to the diversity of film distribution companies. This implies the calculation and evaluation of the ratio of mainstream, independent and non-commercial film distribution companies. The diversity of film distribution can be measured by making an inventory of the number of releases of blockbusters and art-house films and the geographic reach and density of film exhibition. Flexible programming of a wide range of films, different language versions of films, and 'alternative content' should be facilitated by offering efficient options for realising a smooth traffic in digital files.

Be assured of the basic truth: each distribution company still needs a sufficient number of outlets. The saturation of film exhibition can be charted by assembling statistical information about the supply facts, such as the number of cinemas per capita, or one can explore the area of demand and try to collect data regarding the distance customers need to travel in order to reach a cinema and their degree of willingness to travel. Digitisation of the infrastructure makes it possible to launch a premiere film in all available cinemas. This sounds great, but it predominantly facilitates an increase of saturated releases aimed at a quick turnover. It is possible to intensify this concentration even further to also include the online and DVD release at the same moment. This is called 'Day for Date release', meaning a simultaneous, multiplatform and multi-territory release. Currently, there is a discussion within the film industry about the advantages and disadvantages of this market strategy. Many professionals prefer the cinema release to be earlier than the online release and to maintain the traditional release 'windows'. The adjustments in the commercial practice of a saturated release could be considered as a positive change for small cinemas that formerly had to wait until a 35mm print was available for them. On the other hand, the negative result is that just a few films are screened everywhere, in many cities, even in several local cinemas at the same time. The explanation for this business trend is simple: distributors want to recoup their part of the Virtual Print Fee (VPF) as soon as possible. Fair enough, but this diminishes the diversity of the film programme. In my view, the VPF is most profitable and useful most prominently for mainstream releases. However, there are experiments with a reduced VPF and other tailor made VPF agreements to accommodate small cinemas and independent releases.

## The three chains of film distribution

Film distribution is traditionally the strategic pivot point in what, in terms of business administration, is called the 'supply chain' of the film industry. From a logistical perspective, distribution is the connecting link between production and exhibition. Distribution companies are part of a network that consists of the film crew, sales agents, film festivals, film theatres and the cinema audience.

Film distribution is also part of a 'value chain', a complex network of film circulation built upon a delicate balance of economic interests. This network could be mapped by making an inventory of business contracts and an analysis of corresponding indicators. A film distributor invests in the purchase of the screening rights for a certain territory during a certain time for one particular film, anticipating rental revenues from the cinema owners. The aim of a film distributor is to mediate between the extensive supply and the specific demand, working with a certain mixture of artistic vision and economic sensibility. It is essential for a film curator to have more than basic knowledge of both the supply chain and the value chain, because these business conditions influences the artistic possibilities. Further details about the financial and juridical structures of the international film distribution are to be found in Cones (2002), Acland (2003), Iordonava (2008), Parks (2012), Elberse (2013) and Ulin (2014).

Even in the digital age, film distribution still largely determines which films are to be seen where, by whom and under what circumstances. The choices of the film distributor are decisive for which films come into circulation. Film distribution is therefore a critical node in the network that underlies the global exchange of viewing experiences. For non-commercial distribution the selection is based on the passionate urge to spread film art, but for commercial distribution the main strategy is to circulate cultural commodities in the most profitable and efficient way, minimising risks and aiming for optimal revenues. In both cases, film distribution is an influential link in what art sociologists call the 'decision chain'.

*Informal film distribution*

The Australian media researcher Ramon Lobato (2012) argues that there should be academic attention paid to the film trade that exists outside of institutional channels of governments and independently of the international media corporations. This subject is still a largely uncharted territory within research programmes of film studies. Lobato focuses on an international inventory and analysis of the contemporary informal and non-theatrical distribution of films. He indicates a fundamental problem for doing research in this field: informal film distribution is an industry that is, by definition, not documented and therefore difficult to collect data about. Its exact turnover is difficult to measure and even the most elementary details of this shadow economy are not available. Still, he argues that informal film distribution should be put on the research agenda; firstly because it represents a large proportion of the film trade, secondly because it has a significant cultural impact.

One of the most basic questions in film studies is to make an inventory of the different manners of access to film culture: which films are being watched by which audience with what kind of consequences? Lobato phrases this as follows: 'Contexts of distribution – where, how and when people encounter movies – frame the perceived meaning of texts and the way we incorporate them into our symbolic lives' (2012: 17–18). He argues that in search of an answer on this matter one cannot ignore informal film distribution. Indeed, a large and growing number of film consumers watch films intensively but never visit a cinema or film festival. Viewing habits such as these are generally declared illegal by the established powers, because it amounts to copyright infringement. In his essay 'Six Faces of Piracy', Lobato draws a more nuanced image of this phenomenon. According to him, you could describe piracy as theft, but also as innovative entrepreneurship and co-creation, as an increase in access, as the free exchange of ideas, or as resistance to the power of the big media conglomerates. Informal film distribution is an elusive phenomenon, because it is a form of trade that is fragmented and geographically sparse. Lobato underpins his argument for redefinition of this issue with many examples and a few more detailed case studies, such as the distribution in Brazil of *Tropa de Elite* (*Elite Squad*, José Padilha, 2007). Illegal DVD versions of this popular feature film were available even before its official premiere, but this did not appear to undermine the success of the theatrical release, and perhaps even increased the number of viewers.

Informal film distribution is sometimes closely intertwined with informal film production, as is the case in Nigeria, where the flow of cheaply made video films has given rise to the term 'Nollywood'. This is an autonomous circuit of media circulation that only rarely receives attention outside the country's borders (one such exception was the International Film Festival Rotterdam in 2004). Informal film production also exists in the Western world in the form of unprestigious genre films that are produced in series and made according to fixed formulas. This is the domain labelled infamously as 'straight to video'. Lobato signals cheerfully that these films are indeed utterly predictable and mediocre, but this should be valued as a positive quality. It is a shadow economy and a subculture that he believes should be considered as a central part of global film culture. He compares it with the characteristics of the output of the 'Poverty Row' producers during the golden decades of the Hollywood studio system.

In his view, the majority of film researchers target their investigations too much on canonical films and limit themselves to analysing topics such as text structures, narrative strategies or personal style. He also observes that the current research of the film industry is focused mainly on the historical economic background of the generally recognised corpus of films. He acknowledges that over the years the film canon has become more diverse, and several academics are paying more attention to a variety of niche markets of cult movies and the history of various cinematic subcultures, but according to Lobato the aim of this kind of research remains restricted to the ambition to disclose the hidden quality and cultural value of the films scrutinised. Lobato argues that informal film distribution is difficult to grasp within this traditional point of view and advocates a broadening of the theoretical framework in the direction of the paradigms of social geography,

37

urban studies, cultural economics and media anthropology. He presents his research modestly as a minor case study fitting into a larger project of investigating social and cultural practice. In his closing chapter, Lobato makes a clear inventory of the different forms of this grey area of digital traffic and communication. He ends with a positive statement: media consumers can be more than just passive observers and can instead acquire the position of focused and well-grounded commentators.

Future film historians (and film curators) might be curious what kind of developments in media practice took place in the first decade of the twenty-first century and how contemporary academia reflected these changes happening around them. Ramon Lobato offers a solid starting point for charting this kind of investigation. In the last few years, the Internet has rapidly become the main transit zone for the circulation of films; see also Dina Iordanova and Stuart Cunningham (2012).

### 3.2 Copyright: A Blessing or a Curse?

There is no such thing as a free screening. As a film curator you are inevitably confronted by the issue of rights clearance, which means you have to acquire the formal permission to show a film in a public screening. Clearing the rights for showing a film in your programme is a constraint for every film curator. If you present just recent releases then the distribution companies take care of this task, but if you intend to present film heritage you are most of the time on your own, facing a complex search finding the rights holders. But above all you are confronted by the question: what is a fair fee? Prices can vary enormously, from a reasonable compensation of costs by film archives to very unreasonable fees by commercial companies.

A film curator has to define his position in the debate concerning the dichotomy between the protection of Intellectual Property (IP) versus freedom of cultural exchange. This discussion has gained topicality and urgency with the advent of the Internet. Copyright is a legal grey area. Firstly because film is a global phenomenon and copyright legislation is still a matter of national concern, despite the attempts for more unification by the World Intellectual Property Organization (WIPO) of the United Nations. Secondly, it can be difficult to determine just who is the legitimate holder of copyright for films. Generally the producer is considered the rights holder, but they can sell these rights for profit, or lose them as result of bankruptcy or mergers. The core questions are: What is the right balance between legal and financial justice for the producer and unobstructed accessibility of the work? What conditions regarding the free availability of films ('creative audiovisual content') are reasonable? You could rephrase this as, what do we understand by 'fair use' of films? Fair use has become a commonly used legal term that is not clearly defined. There is a dispute about what is reasonable consent, because there are many opposing perspectives of individual, public and corporate interests.

The clearance of screening rights is relatively easy in cases when there is a distribution firm that releases the film. Copyright of cinema files is nowadays protected by digital encryption and access is secured by sending separate Key Delivering Messages (KDMs). This proves still to be a bottleneck in the workflow of cinemas, but it should be possible to resolve these kind of practical problems soon. A more essential point is that a resourceful film curator does not limit himself to the current releases, because in composing a truly interesting cinema programme he needs to have the opportunity of an unlimited choice of relevant film repertoire and film heritage to be used as counterpart or addition to the harvest of the day.

The Academy Award-winning animation *Father and Daughter* (Michael Dudok de Wit, 2000), for instance, is a worthwhile addition in several possible ways, either as a short before feature films or as part of a compilation. This film was made available on YouTube by many people, which can be seen either as a sign of respect and enthusiasm, but also loss of income and loss of control for the creator. If you want to show this film in your cinema for a large audience, you could easily download the film from the Internet without giving any notice, or you could investigate where you can get the formal permission for the screening. The latter option is naturally the proper thing to do, but what can you expect when you do?

If you make enquiries about screening rights the best outcome would be that the film belongs to the public domain, because this means one can screen the film for free. However, more often you are confronted by two options: either nobody knows who to address (for this category the term 'orphan films' is used), or somebody states that he is the holder of the rights and usually demands a huge fee for permission to screen the film. In the USA a whole industry exists whose core business is the 'renewal' of the copyright of Hollywood movies. David Pierce (2007) discusses how complex and whimsical this specific legal business can be.

For film archives, respecting copyright is a delicate issue, because with an unregulated use of their archival film material they would lose their necessary reliability to their stakeholders. Therefore, every film archive will be very cautious in granting permission for screenings of the films from their collection. The primary condition for receiving film prints is the guarantee that nobody is permitted to gain illegal profit by presenting these films. This is the reason why every respectable film archive demands that you should settle the permission for screening with the right holders. If there are no known right holders, you should prove that you have made 'reasonable efforts' to trace them and also sign a 'letter of indemnity', which is a sort of disclaimer stating that you guarantee to settle the payment of a screening fee in case a right holder does turn up.

As an alternative to complex and costly legal disputes, initiatives like 'creative commons licensing' are developed. It advocates 'open access' by means of informal self-regulation of free traffic of films and other forms of intellectual property. The producer allows free circulation of his creation on conditions such as non-commercial use, no permission to make any changes, and to provide proper source credits. Another strategy is to defy all limitations of copyright by ignoring authorisation. A good example of best practice of this rebellious option is the website of Jerry Murbach (doctorMacro.info), offering a wide choice of precious film publicity photos and stills in high resolution, as a welcome addition to the regular publicity photos. Still, you could argue about the status of this initiative: is this facilitation of free access a sign of anarchy, or truly open democracy?

The unauthorised screening of films is often described as 'piracy'. As mentioned in the previous section, Australian media scholar Ramon Lobato made a plea for a more nuanced judgement about piracy. American film scholar Peter Decherney argues that there should be a balance between the interests of copyright holders and users:

> Since the days of Edison, overly aggressive technological controls have alienated customers and driven them to piracy. Digital locks and content filters must be used carefully in order to maintain any effective influence and authority. Technology may have altered the everyday administration of copyright, but the fundamental principles that allow the system to function remain remarkably unchanged. (2012: 235)

The possibilities to reach the ideal situation of a free global sharing of knowledge and cultural goods is dependent on several forces, such as state authority, the mechanisms of market competition and the protection of private property. Inevitably, there is a clash of conflicting interests. A variety of obstructions, limitations and even intimidations are unfortunately common practice in the arena of copyright. In this book we ignore the issues of copyright concerning home cinema because the focus is on the public screening of films. From this perspective there is a need to open up legal possibilities in order to realise a greater diversity of films on offer. It seems to be a noble cause to bypass the one-dimensional pursuit of profit of big media corporations and other commercial parties. It is also brave to contest strict censorship by repressive state authorities. Free trade of cultural goods would indeed improve the smooth accessibility to film repertoire and film heritage, but on the other hand, for the individual or corporate right holders this means the loss of possibly justified control and unjust loss of revenue.

In short, the domain of copyright is still fraught with many pitfalls. We have to choose between protection of the intellectual property of film producers and the possibility of free access to film art. If you do the right thing and clear the rights legally for each screening of unreleased films, these screenings are difficult to make profitable to the extent that it may even be impossible to recover the costs involved. Yet there is a large loss of income in the film industry due to informal distribution and illegal circulation (aka piracy). On the one hand copyright legislation clearly obstructs the scope of choice for film curators but on the other it also has proven to facilitate the traffic of films. In this perspective, copyright is to be considered as both a blessing and a curse.

### 3.3 An Exploration of Flm Criticism

Naturally, a film curator should be able to write alluring and insightful programme notes, reasoned catalogue texts and tempting press releases, in order to contextualise their programme and to present his potential audience with a trustworthy recommendation or informed analysis. A film curator should be able to motivate his choice and convince his audience of his arguments. The best thing is to practice as often as possible and to analyse best practices (Timothy Corrigan [2006] offers the best guidance for writing this kind of film criticism). This section explores the phenomenon of film criticism further.

A film curator is part of a ritual of creating reputations, partly out of unselfish idealism in supporting the flourishing of quality films, partly out of enlightened self-interest to support the successful presentation of these films in the public arena of festivals, theatres or archives. Professional film criticism is an independent part of this reputation chain, sometimes as partner of the film curator, sometimes as opponent. The resemblance between the two crafts is that both need an audience: film critics need readers (who may never go to see the film), curators need visitors (who might not have read the reviews). The possible similarity between the tasks of a professional film critic and a film curator is that both experts are attempting to provide relevant information to situate a film in its context and to propose structures of reflection, to reveal diverse relations of similarities and connections, to formulate value concepts and to construct criteria of judgement. All this in order to motivate the importance of discoveries, to select outstanding achievements and to defend these choices, to provoke discussions about interpretations and to express articulate opinions about quality and excellence. Here follows an exploration of film criticism, seen from the perspective of film curating:

> Writing about film can serve one or several functions. It can help you ... understand your own response to a movie better; convince others why you like or dislike a film; explain or introduce something about a movie, a filmmaker, or a group of movies that your readers may not know; make comparisons and contrast between one movie and others, as a way of understanding them better; make connections between a movie and other areas of culture in order to illuminate both the culture and the movies it produces. (Corrigan 2006: 6).

### Every film needs a buzz

In the digital age there is a massive flow of amateur film criticism, surfacing as user comments, posts on social media platforms, blog texts or reviews and essays. At the end of this chapter we explore this phenomenon in more detail. First we investigate the three modes of professional film criticism, labeled as 'journalistic criticism', 'essayistic criticism' and 'academic criticism' (Bordwell 1989: 20), or 'movie reviews', 'critical essays' and 'theoretical essays' (Corrigan 2006). These three categories can be distinguished from each other by their different context. A film review normally has a news context (daily paper, news magazine, radio, television, website); examples are provided by portals like IMDb.com (Internet Movie Database), Rottentomatoes.com or MRQE.com (Movie Review Query Engine). A film essay is usually situated in a medium aimed at a specific taste group; they are published in books or film magazines, printed or online. A film analysis typically has a scientific surrounding (peer reviewed journal, books, educational courses). Recently, the genre of video lectures, or audio-visual essays, has increased in prominence and scope. For an overview and reflection on this topic, see the first issue of *Frames Cinema Journal* (2012). These three different contexts translate into different target audiences of readers and different sets of style and tone of voice. More essential is the difference in application of a theoretical frame and the intentions of the critic. A film review is an unbound argument surfacing as a fluid flow of description, interpretation and grading: a review offering in essence a mix of personal observation and evaluation. In contrast, a film essay has a more outspoken critical perspective, a more solidly built argument of greater length, and film analysis is the result of a scientific research and is therefore placed in the context of a scientific method, such as, for example, 'Neo-Formalism' (Thompson 1988) or 'Poetics of Cinema' (Bordwell 2008). For more possible critical perspectives see Hollows and Jancovich (1995), Hill and Church Gibson (2000) or Furby and Randell (2005).

All three modes of professional film criticism mentioned above are characterised by two main tasks: interpretation and evaluation. The competence of critical interpretation is rooted in a long historical tradition of hermeneutics. In his book *Making Meaning* (1985) David Bordwell gives an overview and a critique of the phenomenon of hyperbolic interpretations offered in some branches of film studies. In a blog post of August 2014 he argues that there is no direct connection between mass entertainment and zeitgeist, as is often stated. In his view, it is highly unlikely that mainstream films somehow reflect its surrounding society. Therefore, *Dawn of the Planet of the Apes* (Matt Reeves, 2014) for instance cannot be considered as a clear and perfect intentional metaphor for the conflict in the Middle East, as some critics have suggested. Bordwell explains that this kind of reasoning is corrupted by circular arguments and he offers several alternatives for making meaning of a viewing experience at the cinema (see Bordwell 2014a). Another warning not to indulge into the act of (over) interpretation can also be found in the famous essay by Susan Sontag, 'Against Interpretation' (1963). Her statement still fuels a lively discussion; see, for example, Totaro (2005).

*Analysis of a critical value judgement*

A second aspect of professional film criticism is the critical value judgement, rooted in a long aesthetic tradition characterised by dynamics of re-evaluation and shifting judgements. A frequently discussed subject is the possible impact of film reviews on ticket sales. Extensive research has been carried out on this issue and the conclusions are mostly the same: the recommendations of friends always prove more influential than any review, and the size of the review and the size of the photo clearly create more attention than any elaborate evaluation. Still, it is worthwhile trying to analyse the ways a film critic could build their arguments for their value judgement and apply this analysis also to curatorial decisions. In essence, a film curator is a storyteller, telling a story about the value of films. Each programme concept is based upon critical questions like 'Why is this particular film important', or 'Why is this specific combination of films interesting?' Which criteria and norms did you use? How could you categorise and classify films? To quantify your opinion in five stars or less is a very reductive activity, as it says little about the quality of the film in question. Yet a more elaborate, qualitative critical value judgement often seems elusive or difficult to reason. To formulate a nuanced description and substantiation of a critical opinion remains an eternal challenge.

In my opinion, it is perfectly possible to quarrel about taste, provided that the participants in these discussions do have a sufficient vocabulary and knowledge of argumentation theory. Let's take the following example: the judgement 'This film is good', could be expanded upon with the argument '...because this film is realistic'. The concealed standard or implicit criterion is: '...for all the good movies are realistic'. Of course we know that the term 'realistic' is problematic, and reductive critical judgements of this sort are from the point of view of logical reasoning to be considered as incomplete or even as a complete fallacy. Taste is certainly debatable, but it inevitably begs many questions. A value judgement is indeed taking a personal and possibly polemic position in relation to movies in general and usually one movie in particular. How do you determine the truth of a value judgement that is in essence an explicit subjective understanding of a film? How do you analyse the logic of a critical argument? Which critical standards are defendable, what justifying principles are possible and acceptable, which reasons could one give for the evaluation of quality in films?

The analysis of value judgements can be facilitated by dividing the potential critical criteria into subgroups. A systematic inventory allows us to identify patterns in making judgements about films. This forms the basis for a possible explanation of these judgements. I suggest to distinguish three categories of possible arguments – aesthetic, realistic and emotional.

Critical arguments in an aesthetic perspective are based upon the assumption of film seen as an autonomous art form. Standards for value creation include the degree of craftsmanship, innovative expression, eccentric creativity; clarifying comparisons of stylistic aspects of different films. It is possible to distinguish three standards in the perspective of aesthetics:

1a. The standard of craftsmanship suggests that a movie is good if it is made with visible, professional craftsmanship. 'Masterpiece' is a common term here. The film critic evaluates the qualities of the *mise-en-scène* (staging) and editing, assessing the use of cinematic resources and display of technical skill and examining the narrative composition with criteria such as a tight plot or well-developed characters.

1b. The standard of artistic innovation ('avant-garde') or artistic idiosyncracy ('independence') states that a film is good if it breaks away from tradition, stands apart from the greatest common divider and has a personal tone. Implicit here is often an idea of progress: films must be improving.

1c. The standard of the comparison that a particular film is better or inferior in comparison with other films. The comparison may be based on an observable consistency in terms of film form, between films of the same category (style, period, genre, movement, a body of work, or remakes of the same story), or may be developed on the basis of the personal associations of the film critic. A special case of this standard of value creation is the issue of novel adaptations. A dispute is possible about which version is to be considered better, and also about the relevance of the comparison.

Critical arguments in a realistic perspective are based upon the assumption of film seen as a realistic representation of daily life. Standards of evalution include the degree of probability, abstraction, commitment, ethics. Value creation is based on the degree to which a film is related to the historical or present reality. This includes the question of the influence of the social context, an evaluation of the ideology of the film, assessed within the context of Feminism, Marxism or any other political theory. It is possible to distinguish four standards in the perspective of realism:

2a. The standard of probability (verisimilitude, or *'vraisemblance'*) states that a film is good if it represents a worldview that matches with what is possible or conceivable in real life. In the conversations of the general audience this argument often comes up, for example by criticising anachronistic costumes or other details. One would expect that professional film critics have more intelligence at this point. A film viewer must be able to accept that every film creates its own world and thus its own probability.

2b. In contrast, the standard of abstraction states that a movie is good if the everyday reality is displayed in an abstracted way, meaning that the film elevates the coincidental events and personal experiences to a level of timeless validity.

2c. The standard of engagement states that a movie is good if it makes an explicit, demonstrable commitment to social issues or social justice. In other words, the apparent ideological or political assumptions and implications are acceptable to the critic. An interesting side note is that this critical interpretation does not need necessarily correspond with the intention of the creators of the film.

2d. The standard of ethics states that a film is good if the moral tenor of the film is sound. On the negative side this could include an isolated assessment of the levels of, for example, violence, nihilism, pessimism, profanity or pornography. This way of thinking forms the basis for ranking systems for age verification. In the most extreme form of this prescriptive standard the film should have pedagogical value, or contain disguised life lessons.

Critical arguments in an emotional perspective: where film is seen as fuel for audience response and emotion. Standards of evaluation include the physical reflex and level of identification. The terminology of the emotional criteria consists of words like empathy and euphoria or ecstasy and pathos. Value creation is based upon the psychological effect that the film has upon the viewer. In this case the value judgement on the movie is determined by the mood it evokes, the degree of rapture or fascination of the viewer. In general one can say that the evaluation according to the emotional criteria looks at the mind of the viewer, to the transfer of inspiration, encouragement, hope, fear, fright or tenderness. There seems, oddly enough, to be a taboo on uninhibited emotional surrender to a movie. The emotional criteria seems to be somewhat suspect in critical practice, it has the connotation of a thoughtless revelling in feelings and instinctive reflexes. But this prejudice is not substantiated. It is possible to distinguish two standards in the perspective of emotions:

3a. The standard of physical reflex states that a movie is good when it evokes irresistible emotions, for example produces a laugh ('comic', 'hilarious', 'funny'), or well-being ('feelgood movie'), or generates a tear ('sentimental', 'melodramatic', 'tear jerker'), or causes sweat of anxiety ('horror', 'suspense'), or is sexually exciting ('erotic'). And in negative terms: a film is to be considered bad when the film elicits a nauseating sense of disgust. The most destructive negative value judgement is that the film gives the critic a feeling of boredom or induces drowsiness. It is also possible to recognize intentional enlargements of the emotional appeal of a film, a playful form of irony labeled as 'cult' or 'camp'.

3b. The standard of identification states that a movie is good when film viewers are able to recognise themselves in the movie characters, that they are able to identify themselves with their state of mind and their motivations. A film like *The Lunch Box* (Ritesh Batra, 2013) is appealing to a audience worldwide because of its humanistic and universally appealing portrayal of an encounter between two people brought about by a charming mistake. In other cases, one can argue that the film aims to achieve a deliberate blocking of spectators emotions, the keyword here being 'alienation'.

Please note that the categories presented here are just a tool to trace the variety in the critical evaluation process in order to get a grip on them. Possible questions include: What patterns can be distinguished in the process of critical evaluation? For example, which different forms of indications of probability, or delineations of the avant-garde, or definitions of the exotic? There are more fundamental observations and relativisations to make, in order to round up this inventory in a nuanced way. Firstly, a critical evaluation of films could combine several criteria taken from all of these three groups. For instance, a classic film like *The Grapes of Wrath* (John Ford, 1940) could be valued both in an aesthetic way and as an example of engagement with a social problem. A documentary film like *Five Broken Cameras* (Emad Burnad and Guy Davidi, 2011) could be viewed as both a realistic and activist movie, but also as a compelling story that enforces an emotional response of compassion for the filmmaker, who is living in a colonised Palestinian village suffering from bureaucratic brutalities and intimidations by the Israeli army. Secondly, a critical evaluation can be translated into a curatorial evaluation; a curator of a human rights film festival for instance would combine the criteria of activist ethics and engagement with the criteria of aesthetic quality. Thirdly, my inventory of potential critical criteria of film critics is not exhaustive and the inventory also can be set up differently; for instance if a critic takes into account criteria such as the popularity of the film, or its instructiveness, originality or consistency, or the intentions of the filmmakers. Fourthly, film critics are to be regarded as a special subset of the movie audience. The above criteria can also be used by film curators and members of the film audience (see Carroll 2003). In all three groups, it is evident that behind the process of judgement and appreciation a mostly unspoken story is hidden: the specific details of the person, the context and the motivations of the critic. There is a sliding scale to be drawn – on the one side the imaginary extreme of a total independent rudiment, and on the other the likewise imaginary extreme of a subjective judgement determined by one's social position and social conditions.

And there is the most fundamental question of them all: what is the relevance of a critical value judgement? The answer can be found in the observation that one of the aspects of the context of a critical value judgement is the connection to a collective selection of what films are considered as extraordinary or outstanding. This aspect is called the film canon, a most influential concept.

*The film canon*

The general discussion of canon formation in the art world circles around the definition of widely shared valuations of the cultural past. One option is to highlight the didactic usefulness. In that case the canon is a reasoned shortlist of prime examples of cultural heritage everybody should be familiar with. Another option is to focus on the social value as a shared agreement on the highlights of culture. However, knowledge of the past is never neutral and valuations are by definition subjective. Therefore, compiling a canon will always inevitably lead to a discussion of aesthetic principles.

American film researcher Janet Staiger has discussed the different strategies (or policies) of film scholars in the formation of the film canon. Initially, their strategy was aimed at the recognition of the medium of film as an art form ('politics of admission') but in due time it became necessary to develop criteria for the selection of a core group and the composition of a hierarchy ('politics of selection' or 'politics of inclusion and exclusion'). Staiger suggests that the formation of a film canon is embedded in a larger network of influential factors. She discusses the role of film scholars and the choice of films in their courses and emphasises the role of authority ('politics of power'). The formation of a film canon depends on what is considered as valuable and this depends on which voice has the most authority. Staiger poses the following questions:

> By what standards do we make value judgements? What are the political implications of various standards? What ends do these standards promote? How do we, if we are to make selections based on value, choose among the standards? If evaluative standards are for the social good, who determines the social good? Are standards for the society at large, for segments of the society, for individuals? What about those outside a particular hegemonic culture? (1985: 11)

The British magazine *Sight and Sound* can be seen as a trendsetter in the area of canon formation in the film world. In 1952, the first survey to find the top ten films of all times was conducted among film critics and other connoisseurs. This survey has been repeated every ten years, consequently gaining a great reputation, and has been subject of many discussions (see among others Wollen [1993], Sallitt [2002] and Totaro [2003]). One could argue that nowadays there are many canons, for children films, documentaries and experimental films, etc. Virtually each genre of narrative film has its own gallery of 'classics', accepted by various taste groups.

*Conclusion*

Nowadays there is a crisis on the supply side of professional film criticism, because there is a lack of funding. There is also a crisis on the demand side, because there is a lack of readership and attention. For an elaboration on the current state of affairs in film criticism, see Frey (2014) and Frey and Sayad (2015). Professional film criticism therefore seems to limit itself to two modes: on the one hand the specialist or elitist academic essays and on the other the accessible or simplistic film criticism in blogs and user comments. The existence of a middle ground of extended, reasoned reviews seems to be in danger. Plain personal and populist film criticism is gaining in importance. Everybody can release unfiltered and largely unedited opinions about films on a wide choice of forums, or create a private platform and start a blog. The movie review becomes an ego-document or a means of personal branding. There is a danger of superficiality and triviality in this crowd sourced communication, as phrased by among others Andrew Keen in his book *The Cult of the Amateur* (2007). In my opinion, a flourishing film culture needs an independent, dedicated and engaged professional film criticism. A film curator has a responsibility to support the realisation of this ideal. One of the reasons to do this is self-interest, because a film curator has the opportunity to select the best pick of both professional film criticism and user comments, and use citations or links to promote his programme and interact with his audience. All films need an audience. Some films need an acquired taste.

The end of this chapter concludes our general introductory observations on film curation. We have laid a solid fundament for the investigation of curating films. The next three chapters give a brief overview of the core of the subject: what are the specifics of curating film theatres, film festivals and film archives?

# 4     CURATING FILM THEATRES

This chapter contains an initial draft for identifying possible curating strategies, sketched with a film theatre in mind, but also applicable for film festivals and film archives. The central issues are the identification of the various options for constructing a film programme and an exploration of the role of the cinema audience.

## 4.1 The Programme

The task of distribution companies is partly curating the film programmes for a whole territory. If your film programme exists only of a set of newly released films, in first run or second run, then you are not a film curator or programmer but a scheduler of screenings. It is a respectable job and a craft that needs a lot of experience. You need to know the films and also to know your audience. Your task is to find an audience for each film, one as large as possible. A film curator thinks the other way around: he is searching out films for an audience, as many films as possible within the given setting. A film curator evidently also needs to know his audience, but his starting point is different. In practice, there are many mixed forms combining releases with 'speciality' programming. The supply of new releases is essential for a sound business model of the industry. In combination with a creative and well-argued self-curated programme, the artistic diversity can be guaranteed.

A first distinction is between the extremes of a fully public-oriented choice and solely artistically motivated choices. What kind of evaluative 'Key Performance Indicators' (KPIs) do you agree upon: achieving the highest possible box-office results, or creating the best possible programme? This coarse dichotomy could be elaborated in a set of more detailed and nuanced overviews of possible intentions. Intentions can be translated into qualitative 'Critical Success Factors' (CSFs), in order to define the identity of your vision and the criteria you have determined. In this way it is possible to formulate in a measurable way the focus you have chosen and to motivate most precisely the relevance and authenticity of your programmes. Some examples of qualitative critical success factors:

- 'Popularity' – giving priority to achieving the best possible match between the supply of films and the demands of the audience.
- 'Social engagement' – aiming at involvement with a social purpose and outreach to the audience.
- 'Diversity of audience' – aiming at different segments and taste groups.
- 'Diversity of films' – aiming at the widest possible choice of films, presenting a representative sample of the available supply of films.
- 'Uniqueness' – focusing on offering films that have the greatest possible degree of rarity, unveiling films which are rarely seen or which are unjustly unknown and forgotten.
- 'Excellence' – presenting the highest artistic quality of cinema, measurable in degrees of craftsmanship, or innovative style. Historical examples are documented in MacDonald (2002) and Hagener (2007).

This set of intentions could be transformed into your own personalised scorecard to assess your particular strategy of curating. A film programme can be reviewed on the basis of relevant quantitative key performance indicators. A selective inventory of yearly key figures can serve as quantitative assessment criteria: What number of screenings? What number of visitors, in total and on average per screening? What are the total box office results, and what is the average revenue per screening? What are the total costs, and on average per screening? What developments can be seen in these figures? An essential question is whether the scope of your ambition and the size of your programme does fit the available properties of your organisation. This crucial internal analysis can be extended with a critical inventory of the external impact of the programme: what kind of appreciation of public, press, peers and staff is visible? What are the numbers regarding customer loyalty, customer acquisition, customer satisfaction? In addition, another curatorial aspect could also be taken into account: the amount of contextual content given, the degree of possible added value offered through interviews, lectures, seminars, workshops and publications. The evaluation can be completed with an analysis of the positioning of the programme: What are the distinctive features compared with the programming of the competition and the leisure sector at large? What are the unique selling points in a demand-driven market?

Promoting your programme involves fuelling curiosity, awakening expectations, causing a buzz or 'word of mouth'. This is the task of the marketing department, but the film curator can contribute, for example by assisting with marketing tasks such as organising press releases and press conferences, and cooperate by reflecting on the best use of marketing tools, such as the use of trailers (both in the screening rooms and on the website), posters, advertisements or discount promotions. As a curator you could organise special public events such as sneak previews and premieres, with or without extras such as a Q&A with directors and actors, or talk shows, or lectures. The marketing department is responsible for optimal corporate communication, both in print and online, a film curator should be able to give advice to create a variety of public screenings, educational screenings or programmes based on collaborations with other cultural organisations. The cinema venue and the programme, and even the name of the film curator, can thus be made into a 'brand': a well-known and respected quality label that has positive associations and a promotional effect. However, this kind of reputation is not easy to establish.

Seen from a broad perspective, constructing a programme means constructing a sequence of events, either during one-time slot (compilation programme), or one evening (double bill), or a week, or a season. The act of curating means to construct in an inventive way a solid coherence between different films. This act is comparable to making a sentence and the theory of communicative functions of the linguist Roman Jacobson could be applied here (see Jacobson 1960). Curating film implies thinking along two axes: the axis of selection ('paradigmatic') and the axis of combination ('syntagmatic'). *Selection* means choosing the content of each unit. There is a wide scope of options available: do you select a short film or feature film, a fiction film or documentary, live action film or animation, mainstream or experimental, local or international? *Combination* means choosing a strategy for constructing a motivated chain of connections.

The artistic choice of the curator could be based roughly on three main alternatives: either on the intention to offer clear contrasts and to evoke interesting collisions, or on the search of similarities, aiming to offer precise matches in mood and style, or to offer a series of free associations. In all these cases a curator is constructing meaning and adding value through creating a mutually supportive sequence. The whole is greater than the sum of it parts.

The act of curating is also comparable with film editing. In my view it is insightful to apply the Montage Theory of Sergei Eisenstein to curating cinema (the concepts of this theory are explored in Aumont 1987). A film curator could choose the principles of a 'dialectic montage', or a 'montage of attractions', or an 'intellectual montage' as a general guideline for his approach. Here follows an elaboration on all three options.

A 'dialectic curatorial strategy' could be achieved by combining contrasting films, resulting in a new level of understanding. For instance the combination of *Women Without Men* (Shirin Neshat, 2009) and *Shirin* (Abbas Kiarostami, 2008) could be interesting, because both films offer an artistic impression of the situation of Iranian women in society, albeit in distinctive different ways. A second option could be to combine *Mogari no mori* (*The Mourning Forrest*, Naomi Kawase, 2007) and *A Single Man* (Tom Ford, 2009), because these very different films have as a common theme the detailed visualisation of the grieving process. A third example of a set of contrasting films could be to offer a double bill consisting of *Gerry* (Gus Van Sant, 2002) and *Into the Wild* (Sean Penn, 2007): both films show in a different way young men confronted by landscapes of wilderness and existential emptiness.

A 'curatorial strategy of attractions' could consist of combining highly diverse screenings with a mixed programme of interludes and surprises such as short films, installations and performances of artists, live music in various forms, all set in a context of cheerful fringe phenomena such as market stands in your lobby, cocktail bars and tapas. One option is to recreate the cinema of attractions of early times (see Strauven 2006).

An 'intellectual curatorial strategy' could be reached by combining two films that can be conceptually linked to each other. For instance, the image of a person circling at free will around on a moped could be the connecting link between the Swiss film *Les petites fugues* (*Small Escapes*, Yves Yersin, 1979) and the Belgian film *La Promesse* (*The Promise*, Jean-Pierre & Luc Dardenne, 1996). There is an obvious difference in film style, and bare facts such as the age of the protagonists and other story details, but both films convey a strong sense of suppressed rebellion.

Curating film also means scheduling screenings in the best possible way. This seems to be an easy and practical issue, but it could however be a decisive factor in the amount of visitors one attracts. Film exhibition has its own concept of prime time. Traditionally, Friday night and Saturday night screenings attracts the biggest crowds. It is possible, however, to create additional rush hours through appealing to a target audience. In this way, a midweek afternoon screening can have the most visitors of the week. The most fundamental choice is between fixed programming, scheduled on monthly basis, and flexible programming, based on weekly prolongation decisions. Do you choose a series of fixed screenings planned long in advance, or do you choose a series of screenings planned by week depending on the ticket sales of each weekend? This decision also has financial consequences, because fixed screenings are regulated by negotiated fees, whereas flexible screenings imply an agreement to split the gross box office based on a sliding percentage.

There is also a distinction to be made between 'horizontal' programming and 'vertical' programming. These concepts are derived from the broadcast practice of scheduling programmes for a television channel. Horizontal programming on a practical level means the coordination of the starting time of each screening in a cinema with several screening rooms. Do all shows start at the same time, or are they spread out in consecutive order? Vertical programming indicates the alignment of several screenings by screening room. A film curator is aware that a matinee, early evening and late evening show attract different audiences and also that each screening room has a specific size and ambience. This knowledge forms the basis for his decisions. There are more practical issues to be considered. Scheduling screenings implies, for instance, also planning enough time between two shows for audiences to leave and arrive and for the staff to clean the room if necessary. On the level of content, we speak of a 'sandwich programme' when popular, accessible films are combined with more unruly, rebellious films aimed at a niche audience. Size matters in this respect: the number of screening rooms and the number of seats in each room defines the range of possibilities for a film curator. A 'megaplex' has more than 16 screens, a 'multiplex' has 8 to 15 screens, a 'miniplex' has 2 to 7 screens, a 'single screen cinema' has, as you may have guessed, just one screen.

*Some options for choosing an artistic criterion as basis for curating a thematic film programme*

A first strategy to label your film programme can be to choose for selecting names of persons taken from the crew and cast, or countries. This first thematic approach focuses on the production side of films.

To take the name of the director as the label for a programme implicitly or explicitly indicates the conviction that a film director has a recognisable personal style and can be seen as the 'author' of the film (see Gerstner and Staiger 2013). This supply of five films would be perfect for a week's programme or a film analysis weekend. The most rewarding job for a curator is to cause renewed attention to filmmakers who have disappeared into oblivion. Examples of best practice are programmes such as 'The Forgotten Films of Valerio Zurlini', or 'Uchida Tomu: Japanese Genre Master', or 'Michael Curtiz Before Hollywood', which toured festivals and film archives around the world in the first decade of the twenty-first century. This approach could be combined with specific thematic boundaries like 'directors in exile', or 'talent on the move'. The director could also function as guest curator. Wes Anderson, for example, gave the cast of *The Grand Budapest Hotel* (2014) the following films to watch, in order to get them in the mood he wanted: *Grand Hotel* (Edmund Goulding, 1932), *The Mortal Storm* (Frank Borzage, 1940), *The Shop Around the Corner* (Ernst Lubitsch, 1940) and *To Be Or Not To Be* (Ernst Lubitsch, 1942).

Taking the name of an actor or actress as the centre for your programme offers the possible binding idea of focusing on acting techniques, or the changing reputation of movie stars, or ways of representation of characters and stereotypes such as the *'femme fatale'* or the 'tough guy'. A double bill of *The African Queen* (John Huston, 1951) and *The Barefoot Contessa* (Joseph L. Mankiewicz, 1954) would be interesting, because Humphrey Bogart stars in both films (and both were recently restored). Let us indulge in some more name dropping: it would be interesting to search for meaningful combinations within the filmographies of actors like Marcello Mastroianni, Michel Piccoli, Cary Grant or Toshiro Mifune; or actresses like Audrey Hepburn, Jean Seberg, Anna Magnani, Catherine Deneuve or Gong Li.

If you choose for the name the producer of a film, it gives you the opportunity to reflect upon the film culture in a specific period and location, for instance the influence of producer Val Lewton at RKO Radio Pictures in the 1940s in Hollywood. Also other crew members can serve as central persons for a programme, for example the director of photography (DoP), or the composer of the film score. The Internet Movie Database (IMDb.com) offers abundant documentation of possible persons and films.

Names of countries of production are popular labels, but offering an overview of a national cinema needs an extensive motivation in order to avoid the danger of arbitrary juxtaposition of totally diverse and incomparable films. One strategy is to choose again an additional theme, something like 'Migration in Europe', or 'South-Korean Costume Films'. Other options include to take a specific category such as 'Japanese Box Office Hits' or 'British Experimental Films', or to choose a specific period as for example 'Silent Soviet Films', or to limit yourself to a specific region, for instance 'The Cinema of the Basque Country'.

Names of cities where the action of the films are located can also function as a thematic denotation for your programme, for example 'Walking Around in Paris', combining films like *Midnight in Paris* (Woody Allen, 2011), *Le Pont du Nord* (Jacques Rivette, 1981), and *Ascenseur pour l'échafaud* (*Lift to the Gallows*).

Another potential strategy is to choose from the existing classifications of films for a foundation for your programme: there is a wide choice of recognised and theorised genres, film movements and film styles.

The range of traditional film genres consist of, among others, westerns, horror movies, musicals, science-fiction films, gangster films, costume films, melodrama, comedies and road movies, each of them with a range of subgenres. For an elaboration on this see Altman (1999), Grant (2007), Wells (2000) and Jeffers McDonald (2007). This genre-focused approach could be combined with specific themes, for example 'Science-Fiction Films and Dystopia' or 'Melodrama and Homosexuality'. A screening of *A Single Man* mentioned earlier, could made more relevant by presenting some Hollywood melodramas from the 1950s characterised by a repressed or hidden representation of homosexuality, as in *A Cat on a Hot Tin Roof* (Richard Brooks, 1958), or the films of Douglas Sirk starring Rock Hudson. Retrospective reflection on this issue can be found in the homage *Far From Heaven*, or the documentary *The Celluloid Closet* (Rob Epstein and Jeffrey Friedman, 1995) and the found footage film *Rock Hudson's Home Movies* (Mark Rappaport, 1992). To top it off, you could add more experimental melodrama's such as *Die Bittere Tränen der Petra von Kant* (*The Bitter Tears of Petra von Kant*, Rainer Werner, Fassbinder 1972) or *Der Rosenkönig* (*The Rose King*, Werner Schroeter, 1986). For a wider overview of melodrama see Mercer and Shingler (2004). There are also several more loosely defined genres, like 'road movies'. In these cases it is possible to be creative with labels of your own imagination. You could for instance divide road movies into a category of  philosophically inclined examples, such as *Im Lauf der Zeit* (*Kings of the Road*, Wim Wenders, 1976), and more light-hearted modes, such as *Little Miss Sunshine* (Jonathan Dayton and Valerie Faris, 2006).

Film movements could be divided in two groups. There are film movements that are connected to specific periods, such as German Expressionism, French Poetic Realism, Italian Neorealism, American film noir, French New Wave. And there are film movements that surface through time, for instance surrealism. A classic example such as *Un chien andalou* (Luis Buñuel and Salvador Dalí, 1928) could be combined with a choice of surrealist animation, for instance the films of Polish animator Jan Lenica and early films of Walerian Borowczyk, or films of the Czech animator Jan Švankmajer, or the Belgian animator Raoul Servais. There are also other modes of contemporary surrealism, like the films of David Lynch, starting with *Eraserhead* (1977), and more recently films like *Uncle Boonmee Who Can Recall His Past Lives* (Apichatpong Weerasethakul, 2010) or *Mood Indigo* (Michel Gondry, 2013).

Taking 'film style' as a guide line for your film programme implies searching for a set of films with defining characteristics in *mise-en-scène*, cinematography, editing and use of sound (see Bordwell and Thompson 2013, 112–327). Avant-garde films are a label that covers a collection of very diverse films. For a discussion of a range of possibilities to programme the short avant-garde film *De Brug* (*The Bridge*, Joris Ivens, 1928) see Bosma (2009). Other possible perspectives could be 'The Colour Fantastic:

Chromatic Worlds of Silent Cinema', or 'Raise Your Glasses: Staging in 3D', or 'Cinemascope in Black and White'. This last mentioned example was a memorable programme presented by the British Film Institute in the 1990s, sponsored by a champagne brand, with pristine prints of, among others, *The Hustler* (Robert Rossen, 1961).

A third strategy for labeling a film programme is to think up a subject-related theme, connected to the reception side of films. Childhood memories are a favourite theme, ranging from tender reminiscences to grim retrospectives. You could think of contrasting *The Tree of Life* (Terrence Malick, 2011) with *Boyhood* (Richard Linklater, 2014). Or to position *An Angel at My Table* (Jane Campion, 1990) alongside the trilogiy of Bill Douglas (*My Childhood*, 1972; *My Ain Folk*, 1973; *My Way Home*, 1978) and the bitter melancholic memories of Terence Davies in *Distant Voices, Still Lives* (1988) and *The Long Day Closes* (1992).

The theme of vengeance of treason or abuse deals with one of the fundamental human emotions. Many westerns are built upon this basic feeling. The story of vengeance can be reassuring if the revenge is completed before the end of the movie and the bad one is finished in style. *High Noon* (Fred Zinnemann, 1952) or *Once Upon a Time in the West* (Sergio Leone, 1968) are famous examples of this kind. The vengeance story can also be disturbing if it is not clear who is the good guy and who is the bad guy. At the end of the film the moral distinctions are opaque, like for instance in moral westerns as *The Searchers* (John Ford, 1956) or *Unforgiven* (Clint Eastwood, 1992). There are many other outstanding films from Hollywood about revenge, for instance *Point Blank* (John Boorman, 1967) or *Ulee's Gold* (Victor Nunez, 1997). The theme of revenge is universal; watch, for example, the Korean feature *Chinjeolhan geumjassi* (*Lady Vengeance*, Chan-wook Park 2005) or the Japanese feature *Unagi* (*The Eel*, Shohei Imamura 1997).

The confrontation of film with experiences derived from other arts is a popular theme that can result in fascinating options for comparative views and cross media projects. Crossmediality means that sometimes a surprising cross-pollination of creativity occurs, whereby the curator functions as a kind of industrious bee. In this case, curating consists of creating interesting encounters between cinema and, for exemple, painting, photography, architecture, fashion, music, theatre, or literature. Abstract animation films belong to a richly filled sub-category that is formed by the overlap between cinema, painting and music. One example is the short film *Motion Painting no 1* (Oskar Fischinger, 1947). In combination with the feature film *Chronik der Anna Maria Magdalena Bach* (*Chronicle of Anna Maria Magdalena Bach*, Jean Marie Straub and Danièle Huillet, 1968) this short film would form a thought-provoking programme dedicated to the use of the music of Johann Sebastian Bach in cinema. His music is overwhelming and confusing, paradoxical. He builds complex structures of chords and variations, but still the overal impression is crystal clear. His music seems to be build on a stern logic and analysis, but its effect is emotional. How do you transpose this into a movie? Directors Straub and Huillet have chosen the perspective of the second wife of Bach. She kept a diary of her daily life with this genius and their many children. Her observations are rendered in a continuous voice-over combined with black and white images. The film style is in accordance with the music style: minimalistic and temperate. It is if you are visiting the home of the Bach family. He has a lot of sublime music written for her and the children, as exercises for them. You see and hear Bach as a dedicated composer, choir leader and family man.

These options are a few established and respectable starting points for a first round of brainstorming. In order to be able to curate a distinguished cinema programme it is most useful to explore the historical and current track records of prestigious cinema venues in several territories, be it film theatres, festivals or archives. Their programme notes and catalogues contain many examples of best practices of creative curating. Some examples of taking further steps to a level of creative curating are also given in the two case studies in chapter seven. The first elaborates on promoting and programming the German silent film *People on Sunday* (Robert Siodmak, Edgar G. Ulmer and Rochus Gliese, 1930). The second case study deals with the example of curating a film exhibition and corresponding screenings in a film archive.

When you construct a programme, your imagination can be boundless. The sky is the limit, provided that you are able to attract an audience for it. However, be aware that the audience proves to be a largely unpredictable variable in the business of film exhibition. The issue of reaching out to target groups and stimulating interaction with your visitors is the subject of the next section.

## 4.2 The Audience

James H. Pine and Joseph Gilmore (1999) introduced the notion of 'experience economy'. Economic values can be connected to commodities (agrarian economy), products (industrial economy), services (service economy) or experiences. Film exhibition can be considered as both a service (a film is screened) and an experience (the screening is a memorable event). There is a range of different domains of customer experience, for instance amusement, education, escapism, or having an aesthetic experience. This customer experience is connected with the customer motivation: what are the expectations of the cinema visitor to go to the movies? Thomas Austin (2007) discusses this issue using a set of recent examples of screen documentaries. For a film curator this context of audience characteristics is important, because there should exist a connection between the programme and the intended audience. However, it is very difficult to formulate the exact nature of this connection and even harder to predict the intensity of it. Audience behaviour and reactions remain largely unpredictable.

Film reception is characterised by a mediated view on three levels. First the camera mediates a view on reality through the recording of photographic images; secondly in the process of editing an imaginary time and space is constructed; thirdly the programme offers a purposeful arrangement of films. Therefore, cinema visitors undergo a triple-mediated gaze. This is the basis of their individual process of showing a response, which can consist of a physical reaction, an interpretation, an evaluation and maybe a vivid recollection. Reception studies is a special division of audience research: it investigates the structure of the cinema audiences, the characteristics of cinema exhibition, and the way visitors react to films. Examples of historical reception studies include Allen (1990), Gomery (1992) and Kuhn (2002). Methodological background is given in Mayne (1993), Staiger (2000), Schröder et al (2003), Stafford (2008) and Biltereyst (2013) among others. For a film curator the knowledge about how films were shown and rated in the past and present can offer inspiration to construct a strategy to please the contemporary audience in your screening room.

Nowadays every film viewer can be his or her own curator, choosing between the many options of available films. The present film culture is characterised by a mixed distribution of films through festivals, theatrical releases, special events, television, DVDs and websites. Movies are displayed on mobile phones, laptops, urban screens and used by VJs at dance parties, but they continue to be seen in the traditional setting of the cinema. The urgent question is raised, why would someone still choose the option to watch a film on the big screen at a specific scheduled moment? This question of motivation directs us to the process of decision-making by the film consumer, who has the luxury of a wide spectrum of possible choices of film consumption. Without an audience, a cinema programme has no meaning. Therefore, it is essential for a film curator to search for responses.

*Some fundamental choices of audience orientation*

Film curators have to reflect upon best practices on the four famous areas of focus on the customers: creating Attention, Interest, Desire, Action (AIDA) in relation to their film programme. A film curator works inevitably together with marketing people. Together they have to make fundamental choices in order to establish an effective marketing strategy within the boundaries of a limited budget and available work force. The first option is to focus on providing a programme for your existing audience and trying to increase the frequency of their visits. The second option is to search for a potential audience and attracting them to your programme. Commercial cinema operates mainly in the frame of service-marketing, which means connecting as specifically as possible with existing popular preferences and needs. If market research indicates that there is a promise of profit, then their market strategy is directed towards catering special interest pro-grammes for specific target groups, for instance ladies nights, workshops for kids, live broadcasts of opera performances, matinees for seniors, or films for ethnic groups. In contrast, art-house cinemas function in a niche market, as they have a target audience that is interested in film art. For a film curator of an art-house cinema the essential questions are: How do we relate to our existing audience and how do we intensify their atten-tion? How can you communicate the urgency to visit your programme? What reasons can you provide to convince also a potential audience to join your target group? The marketing of both venue and film programme is an essential asset of your organisation. Leading questions are: How is your corporate identity perceived by the public, press and peers? What are the motivations of your target group to visit your screenings? There is need for thorough market research and audience research to answer these funda-mental questions. For an overview of relevant marketing theory see Colbert *et al* (2012) and Cashman (2010).

From the perspective of film curating, there is an important audience-related issue of keeping an acceptable quantitative balance in your pro-gramme between the two extremes of too little variation and too much choice. There is also the qualitative counterpart of the delicate balance between the opposing values of giving prevalence to an idiosyncratic per-sonal artistic choice or activist intention, versus adapting oneself totally to the taste of the general audience, focused on an optimal customer satisfaction. Another dual possibility for a way to connect the audience response to your film programme is to make a deliberate choice between opting for either a 'cinema of reassurance' or a 'cinema of disturbance'. The former offers 'feel good movies', films with a positive mood, a happy end and a spirit of optimism. Most of the time it could be labelled as main-stream entertainment, but not necessarily so. Classic examples of high quality in this division are for instance the Hollywood musical *An American in Paris* (Vincente Minnelli, 1951), or the Dutch classic comedy *Fanfare* (Bert Haanstra, 1958). In contrast, 'cinema of disturbance' offers films which confront us with the dark side inside all of us, ranging from films that expresses existential despair, alienation, a feeling of loneliness, or a pessimistic mood, to films which show cruel physical violence and a break down of human civilization. Examples of this category could be found for instance in European art films from the 1970s, like *Last Tango in Paris* (Bernardo Bertolucci, 1972), *Le Locataire* (*The Tenant*, Roman Polanski, 1976) or *Despair* (Rainer Werner Fassbinder, 1978). More recent exam-ples range from the bittersweet melancholia of *Lost in Translation* (Sofia Coppola, 2003) to the grim world of *La Haine* (Mathieu Kassovitz, 1995), *Irréversible* (*Irreversible*, Gaspar Noé, 2002), or *Funny Games* (Michael Haneke, 1997 – remade in the US in 2007).

These choices of taking positions in the spectrum of possible ways of relating to your audience confront us with fundamental dilemmas of curat-ing. Dealing with it requires a thorough knowledge of your audience and the limits of their forbearance: which amount of choice and what kind of offerings can they handle? A film curator should know the habits and tastes of his audience. To get a grip on a very diverse group of cinema visitors, a solid system of segmentation is needed. This means dividing the audience into a set of profiles, based on their mentality and behaviour. What are their preferences, and with what frequency do they visit the cinema? This could be found out in a simple audience survey. But you can go further and investigate if and how your audience wants to interact with you, give feedback or support you. Members of the audience could function as opinion leaders, influencers or 'ambassadors'.

*Know your audience*

A film curator needs to know his audience, because they invest their time and money visiting your programme. Further, a satisfied customer returns, which is essential for a healthy turnover. A crowd of just a handful of attendees could be a rewarding audience, but what is your 'break even' point regarding the number of visitors? What kind of analysis is relevant in the perspective of audience research? By means of the data from your box office computer system you can determine the attendance key figures, both the number of visitors and the number of visits. Statistics of attendance are essential information: Is the outcome in decline, growing or bumping up and down? What is the frequency of their visits, with which interval: each month or week, each Christmas? Next to this neutral, objective data you could research along the line of more subjective parameters, such as what are the barriers your audience encounters before entering your screening rooms, what contextual preferences do they have on the level of service and accommodation? How do they evaluate the programme, how do they grade their experience of the visit and what degree of satisfaction do they score? Which wishes, preferences, desires and needs have they related to the content of your programme, which recommendations to offer? Do they possibly want sneak previews, midnight premieres, Q&As with directors, breakfast screenings, open air cinema, double bills, film professionals as guest curators, retrospectives or seasonal series?

Children (4–12 years) and teenagers (12–16 years) form a special category of audience. There should be a diversity of film choice for this young audience too, because the right to enjoy diversity is not bound by age. Besides the Disney/Pixar releases and other mainstream options there should be an option for the young audience and their parents to decide to watch delightful films from, for instance, Estonia, Denmark, Sweden, Finland, Norway, France, Japan, Germany, China, the Netherlands and many other countries. Children's films have also a canon of classics, minor classics and forgotten masterpieces. For some background and an overview of options in this particular field see Staples (1997), Wojcik-Andrew (2000), Shary (2005) and Lury (2010). The documentaries *A Story of Children and Film* (Mark Cousins, 2013) and *The First Movie* (Mark Cousins, 2009) offer a wide range of inspiration.

You can investigate the profiles of your audience, to make a segmentation of your customers. This implies several actions to undertake. You can make an inventory of demographic aspects such as age and ethnicity, chart geographic aspects such as the distance of their travel to your cinema, and survey socio-economic variables such as wealth and income, and gather relevant contextual data about their consumer behaviour, such as which media they use? More difficult to do is to perform a mentality survey: to try to get a real insight in their psychological identity, to chart their lifestyles and general motivations, to discover patterns in their values and shared interests, grading their scale of involvement and engagement. Which determinants or indicators do you use, how do you measure in a reliable way possible impact? Be aware that there is a clear pitfall in restricting yourself to just formulating or confirming reductive stereotypes.

Each film consumer is looking for intense, unique and exceptional experiences and memories, but the realisation of this desire can take very different forms. On the one hand, there is an extrovert audience that is hunting for fun, ecstasy, a whirl of impressions; on the other, there is a subdued audience that is looking for an aesthetic experience, concentration or reflection, a quiet immersion in emotions and wonder. A film presentation consists of a multifaceted interaction between the audience and the film screen. This is most obviously experienced in the case of comedies. They gain in impact when shown in a crowded room filled with hearty laughter. Furthermore there is also interaction between the spectators themselves. This can work positively, supplementing the individual viewing experience with a cozy togetherness or a strengthening of the evoked feelings, but this interaction could also have negative impact in caste of distraction and annoyance caused by disagreement over how one should behave in a movie theatre.

Segmentation of the crowd on social media could be done by applying the so-called 'Engagement Pyramid', charting online behaviour of your clients. There is a broad basis of passive followers, supplemented by gradually smaller groups of people who share your messages and give comments on them, or produce their own content and own initiatives. The pyramid consists of five possible actions: to like, to endorse, to contribute comments, to produce content, to moderate platforms. Evaluating a film programme could be done by checking the following set of basic key performance indicators of audience participation:

- Access – Does the audience have easy access to film screening, without practical or psychological barriers?
- Attendance – What number of people visit the film screening?
- Involvement – Does the audience show engagement with the screening, do they feel connected to the venue?
- Response – Does the audience react to the screening, either with compliments or complaints, enthusiasm or disappointment?
- Interaction – Does the audience have say on the screening, by means of polls or wish lists?

At the highest level of interaction, the audience acts as a film curator for shows presented on the big screen. This level can be reached by means of 'Cinema on Demand', which is in essence a timesharing concept combined with online crowd ticketing. This format seems to be a promising option for cinemas: firstly, you get a happy audience, because they organised it all themselves, and secondly, you get a low cost, low risk screening, because a sufficiently large audience turnout is guaranteed. Also for film festivals it could be an interesting option to cooperate with a Cinema on Demand portal because they could upload their festival screenings as an additional way of attracting an audience. The traditional perspective of aiming for as many 'bums on seats' as possible now changes into offering the option for bookings of a time slot, conditioned by a critical amount of sold tickets and a choice based on a large, pre-selected assortment of available titles. The conventional top-down programming of entertainment or art films is changed into bottom-up bookings with a personal purpose, or even on community based cinema programming. The industry is sharing the power of the gatekeeper's position with their customers. 'Push' becomes 'pull'. The public becomes the programmer, using social media as communication tool. Examples of cinema on demand are 'Our Screen' (UK), 'I Like Cinema' and 'La Septième Salle' (France), 'Tugg' and 'Gathr' (USA) or 'Moviemobz' (Brazil).

*Conclusion*

Film director Christopher Nolan reflected in a column published in the *Wall Street Journal* in 2014 upon the future of cinema:

> As streams of data, movies would be thrown in with other endeavors under the reductive term 'content', jargon that pretends to elevate the creative, but actually trivializes differences of form that have been important to creators and audiences alike. 'Content' can be ported across phones, watches, gas-station pumps or any other screen, and the idea would be that movie theaters should acknowledge their place as just another of these 'platforms', albeit with bigger screens and cupholders. [...] This bleak future is the direction the industry is pointed in, but even if it arrives it will not last. Once movies can no longer be defined by technology, you unmask powerful fundamentals – the timelessness, the otherworldliness, the shared experience of these narratives.

The notion of shared experience is theoretically explored in Hanich (2014). A shared experience is also at the core of film festivals. The next chapter investigates this field of film presentation.

## 5    CURATING FILM FESTIVALS

Film festivals are popular. This is evident from the fact that they attract large audiences everywhere and there is an extensive choice of international festivals for each day of the year. This ever-increasing popularity raises a lot of fundamental questions, such as what is happening exactly, *how* has this happened, and will it last? Answering and specifying these general questions initiates an interesting discussion, fuelled by fond memories of times gone by, and thoughts on the hypothetical ideal film festival, as well as expectations about the future of film festivals. This chapter offers a brief overview of a few specific issues regarding curating film in the context of the international film festival circuit.

### 5.1 An Exhausting Celebration of Cinema

What makes film festivals so special? In the sociological perspective of the art world, a film festival is to be regarded as an institution where the newest film productions are presented. It has the same function and status as a Biennale in the world of modern art, such as those in Venice, São Paulo or Seoul. A film festival curator could be compared to an art curator and regarded as a gatekeeper who decides what will be selected for display on the international stage. A film festival is a gathering of experts who recognise the earliest signals of new international trends. It is also usually the first platform to launch a film: the commercial circulation of many movies starts here. The question is whether this situation will last, because we live in a time of transition, due to the digitising of distribution and projection. But let us first investigate the position of film festivals at the moment.

The international film festival circuit is the first curatorial phase in the process of global film circulation. Festivals filter the plenitude of film productions and take well-grounded personal taste as the starting point to do so. An essential characteristic of film festivals is an extraordinary alterability. Each edition is to some extent accidental, a more or less happy coincidence of circumstances. The artistic choice depends on the available harvest and the degree of freedom to gather this crop. This seems obvious, but it is still unknown to many outsiders what kind of discouraging obstacles a festival curator has to face, such as the harsh international film trade, the rivalry between festivals, the often unstable funding and variable local cooperation. The big challenge for the festival curator is to succeed in presenting an attractive programme, which is outstanding on the global film festival circuit. Curating for a festival is essentially different from curating for a film theatre or film archive.

> The specificity of festivals is that they need a supply chain that is ongoing yet disrupted. Festivals cannot function as active businesses with continuous operations in the way that traditional film distributors and exhibitors do. The festival is thus an exhibition venue that needs films, but only at a certain time. (Iordanova 2009: 250)

A film festival is in many aspects a challenging 'survival of the fittest'. First of all, it is a stage where reputations can rise, be adjusted or be destroyed. The distinction of 'hot or not' is made under pressures of time and an overload of high quality input. A film festival is a specific kind of microcosm, an isolated setting where film producers, scouts, sales agents, distributors, exhibitors, press and non-professional visitors gather, and so a leading international film festival is a special habitat of travelling films and spectators. Both groups demonstrate a high degree of diversity that is concentrated on a defined location in a very limited period of time. The festival experience therefore stands apart from everyday life and also from regular cinema experiences. The sense of time and space is narrowed down to the festival grounds and festival schedules. The visitors are offered unusual and intense viewing experiences. They perform a collective exploration and celebration of the unknown, digesting the supply of the newest films, exotic surprises, and unfairly forgotten cinema productions. However, participation at a film festival is also a quite peculiar collective exhaustion of both the senses and the body, due to an overload of films and encounters, combined with sleep deprivation and irregular meals. To be allowed to immerse oneself into an overwhelming choice of challenging films is indeed a unique joy and privilege, but can also be a burden and a potential source of anxiety.

The mutual solidarity of festival visitors and guests is expressed in tokens of recognition, such as badges, bags and daily papers. Roughly spoken, festival visitors could be in search of aesthetic pleasure, or immersion in an abundance of films, or seeking glamour (seeing and be seen) or just comfort: no queues at the box office or at the bar or in the toilets, decent catering, not too many last minute changes in the programme, and above all spacious screening rooms with excellent sightlines and perfect projection. A film festival is simultaneously an individualistic search for satisfaction and a social gathering. The profile of the festival visitor is varied; it is possible to distinguish many subcultures in the festival crowds, such as fanatic film buffs, occasional visitors and industry professionals. Each of these different customers aims for a very personal experience of viewings and meetings. 'Cinephilia' could be a dominant and binding element, but it is certainly not the only motivation to visit a film festival. Besides, there are many different sorts of 'cinephilia'; it is a phenomenon with multiple appearances (as is described in chapter two).

The fundamental challenge for the film festival curator consists of dealing with the privilege to get the intense attention and dedication of a lot of different people during several days or a whole week or more. How to please and satisfy them? One option is to specialise in different niche markets of audiences, focusing the selection on the tastes and interests of minority ethnic populations or diasporic communities. Dina Iordanova (2010) distinguishes three possible curatorial purposes in this perspective: to function as a tool of cultural diplomacy, to promote a particular identity agenda, or to explore the economical potential of diasporic events and to foster ethic minority talents.

## 5.2 Branding the Film Festival Experience

The artistic determination needs to be translated into such practical things as a strong logo and appealing graphic design. The marketing of a festival expresses itself also in the facilitation of commercial activities, such as a film market for professionals, a co-production fund, the distribution of festival films and also the offering of educational programmes. A film festival costs money and needs a large budget, but it raises money as well. In the short term, the local economy profits through the increase of tourist business and valuable city marketing. In the long term the film producer sometimes profits through the free publicity for some of the films. Unfortunately, this is by no means predictable, because experience proves that a festival hit is not always a blockbuster at the box office, or may not even be considered for distribution at all.

The 'product' of a film festival is the programme. In order to be able to promote the programme properly it is necessary to create a recognisable 'corporate identity', in other words a clear curatorial profile. This requirement of continuity and recognition is antithetical to the ideals of the programmers, who wish to present a surprising, unpredictable and unique programme for each edition. The 'core business' of film festivals remains the presentation of the best possible programme, selected by a strictly independent staff. The curators and scouts are searching for new discoveries; they select the best quality films of the year, the best of what both the upcoming and established talent has to offer. From the perspective of these artistic choices the essential function of a film festival is the stringent and observant selection of which film is most fit to be presented. Each film festival encourages every promising talent to offer their films, through the procedure of the entry forms. As a result, the festival curators receive a huge number of submissions. In addition to this vast choice the curators do their own research on other film festivals and in the field. Only a few of all these possible options are selected. This procedure is a useful service to the festival visitors: they just need to manage their way through two hundred films instead of two *thousand*. For the curator it is a challenge to explain how this reductive selection has been made. Then again the question regarding the exact profile of the film festival arises; which unique selling points should be mentioned?

A first inventory of possible strategies for curating film festivals could exist of four distinctive aspects which could be objectively assessed. First, the scope of content: choosing between the option of a general selection of new films, or specialising in genres such as documentaries, animation, children films, short films, film heritage, horror films, lesbian & gay films (LGBT), feminist films, or choosing for the option of combining film with other arts (music, dance, photography, modern art, media art). Secondly, the scope of territory of the programme: international, national or regional films. Thirdly, the scope of exclusivity: 'Best of the Fest', or aiming at a high number of world premieres. Fourthly, the scope of target groups: international, national or regional visitors, either industry-focused or audience-directed.

Still, identifying ways of profiling film festivals remains difficult. You could posit the existence of two sorts of curatorial strategies. On the one hand, a film festival curator could focus on films that render an artistic vision and offer a contribution to innovative cinema poetics. An essential characteristic of this view is to favour personal expression, exploring new patterns of temporal rhythms and spatial juxtapositions. On the other, a film festival curator could also choose to compose programmes of films that are expressing persuasive opinions about social problems and offering possible solutions for issues such as the abuse of human rights, disastrous climate change or the destructive food industry. The essential characteristic of this view is creating awareness, engagement, and to reach out to the audience, to stimulate interaction. The primary intention in this case is to question reality through critical research and investigations, in order to raise emotional and rational responses of the festival audience. It is possible to compose a purposeful programme either by reacting on developments and events in society, or take a contrasting strategy by aiming to develop agenda setting programmes, using the juxtaposing of interacting mediated realities and representations as tool of influence.

The distinction between an autonomous artistic motivation and an instrumental activist intention seems to be clear on first sight, but a specification of essentials proves to be more problematic than expected. One could argue that there exists a large overlap between the two views: every curator wants to present quality films and to connect them to the festival audience and the outer world. And all strategies of curating are largely subjective and personal. The selection of films remains therefore a mysterious process. It is an indefinable combination of intuition, idealism and ambition. There is still no clear chart of the influence of curatorial choices and neither of the hidden assumptions and expectations behind it.

## 5.3 Ranking the Festivals

The international film festival circuit is large, therefore strong competition inevitably arises in order to achieve status and attention. Behind the scenes of the festivals a fierce battle rages to attract new discoveries and to present as many films as world premieres as possible and have a sensational opening film and closing event. This arena of sales agents, film producers, film directors, festival programmers and scouts is still not fully explored. The website filmfestivals.com lists thousands of film festivals and provides news and information as completely as possible. The International Federation of Film Producers Associations (FIAPF.org) based in Paris tries to function as a referee regarding the ranking of film festivals, but their authority is not generally accepted. Yet we need some uncontested guidelines for the evaluation of achievements and excellence of film festivals if we want to get a grip on the artistic and social dynamics of the phenomenon of the international film festival circuit.

The easiest way to evaluate the success factors of a film festival is quantitative research: an inventory of diverse ratios such as, for example, the amount of films shown, world premieres, guests received, paying visitors and the amount of press reviews, reports in the blogosphere and reactions on social media platforms. However, these numbers alone are not decisive, because it tells us nothing about the important issue of content assessment. A focus on the qualitative evaluation of the programme would be more interesting: checking the opinions of the festival crowd regarding the perceived quality of the films and clarity of the artistic choices. This is not easy to do. One difficulty for instance is the reliable determination of pre-existing expectations of the visitors (neutral, high or low) and the influence of these expectations in relation to the status of the visitor (film professional or film buff, versed or debutant). There are many forms of customer satisfaction precisely because there are many different sorts of visitors. The challenge for researchers is to develop a survey that can chart the opinions of the audience in a relevant and reliable way. The qualitative evaluation of a film festival could also be done by a forum of experts, instead of conducting an audience survey. This will start a discussion regarding what benchmarks will be appropriate. It is easy to list a few general terms, such as the development of the artistic signature of the festival, the degree of representational coverage of global trends in cinema, the innovative character of the programme, the support of upcoming and proven creative talent and the arousal of the curiosity of potential audiences. To adjust these general terms into measurable criteria is a difficult task though, or even a dilemma which is not yet resolved.

Film festivals constitute an international network of film screenings, but on the other hand each festival is also firmly grounded in a local film culture. The festival staff (and film scholars as well) have to deal with this sliding scale of opposite forces. Another manifestation of a sliding scale of opposite forces is the ambition to present a unique, unpredictable programme in each festival edition and the opposite need for a recognisable, stable artistic signature.

The increasing digitalisation influences the international film culture in many ways. The possibilities of digital worldwide communication undermine the power of the established institutions and requires an adjustment of current curatorial practices, but it also provides more options for a truly independent circulation of films. American film researcher Chuck Tryon placed film festivals in the contemporary context of on-demand culture and digital delivery and investigated the influence of social media on the interaction with festival visitors (2013; 155–72).

## 5.4 Organising Film Festivals

Organising a film festival implies many considerations. Jonathan Gann (2012) offer a series of interviews with a range of (American) film festival curators, covering many practical aspects of the various tasks and challenges behind the scenes. The most fundamental and perhaps most obvious observation to be made is that a festival curator is part of a team. In essence, the management team of a film festival has a dual responsibility: on the one hand to offer an excellent programme supported by a clear corporate identity and effective marketing strategy and on the other hand also to provide for effective fundraising, sound accounting and sophisticated human resource management (see also Tanner 2005).

To start with the last category mentioned: film festival curators and their supporting festival scouts tend to be a bunch of 'free radicals': an independent, high qualified wayward workforce. Still they need to be able to function within the festival team and they need to be supported by firstly a suitable job description, which is formulated as a balanced framework of responsibilities and tasks, and secondly a set of clear procedures of job evaluation. Other HRM issues include distinct and reasonable regulations for recruitment, career development and exit procedures (HRM handbooks as Beardwell and Thompson 2014 offer an overview of options).

Inevitably a film festival engages a vast quantity of volunteers and interns. They form a special category of precious labour force, with particular aspirations and potential. Ideally, their cooperation is a mutually rewarding exchange of give and take, profitable for both parties concerned. The focus is to stimulate their intrinsic motivation, because the pecuniary compensation is minimal or non-existent. For the film festival management the deployment of volunteers and interns provides a unique direct connection to the perceptions of their loyal audiences and the views of upcoming young professionals.

A more practical issue is the fact that the logistics of film festivals are complicated, with a dense traffic of prints, industry guests, guests of honour and visitors. This calls for a perfect workflow planning system. Crowd control is one of the key issues for the festival management. To hire private security and arrange for admission by subscription only is a common practice at the opening nights of virtually all film festivals. But regular festival screenings usually have an open accessibility. The main concern in this case is the operation of unhindered online sales in smooth coordination with box office sales, and to limit the misuse of reservations in order to avoid the combination of empty seats and a large crowd of potential visitors who are not allowed to enter. All this demands a well balanced leadership, covering both artistic and business aspects. A film festival should strive for a transparent cultural governance, based on perfect internal financial control, compliance, risk evaluation and sustainability awareness.

The context of a film festival has in many ways an influence on the organisation of the festival. A first contextual factor is the international film festival circuit. Cooperation with other film festivals is essential to reduce costs and be able to invite big names or compose an extensive programme. The International Film Festival Rotterdam, for exemple, cooperates with both the simultaneously-held Göteborg International Film Festival and the Busan International Film Festival held a half year earlier in the festival calendar. On the other side, there is also the issue of the aforementioned competition between film festivals for the programming of important world premieres. The International Film Festival Rotterdam has a long history of friendly competititve struggles with the closely preceding Sundance Film Festival and the immediately following Berlinale.

A second contextual factor is the issue of censorship, both historical and contemporary. Curators could be confronted with films they want to select but which are censored in their country of origin. In this way, even in open societies film curators can be confronted with restrictions. The affective filmmakers have the choice between the options of compromising with the system of government censorship and accepting cuts or changes, or to use metaphors to express their controversial views in a disguised way, or to accept to perform self-censorship. If their film is still considered in some way offensive, a screening at a foreign film festival is risky. Their film could be banned, or they could even be imprisoned. A curator has a shared responsibility in this situation. Suppose you want to organise an LGBT film festival with a focus on human rights. In many countries this means that you will be confronted by fierce protests, possibly culminating in death threats by intolerant private groups, or indictments by a repressive government. In my view, the necessity of upgrading security protocols means an unacceptable degrading of the required freedom of thought, but on the other hand a film curator should be able to guarantee the safety of his audience, guests and staff. Remember that the Sarajevo Film Festival started amidst the turmoil of a devastating civil war; is this to be considered as a brave defence of civilisation or as an act of dangerous irresponsibility?

A third contextual factor consists of the festival visitors. An audience-directed film festival should have a range of possibilities for interaction and communication. Most festivals have an audience poll, which offers a crude indication of which films are most appreciated. For festival curators it is interesting to check if there are any surprises. Another means of interaction with the audience are the Questions and Answers sessions (Q&As) after screenings. Scott Macaulay (2012) offers concise practical guidelines to deliver Q&As at film festivals. Most of the time, a Q&A with directors or other cast or crew members is set up as a marketing strategy to promote a new film. These tours are expensive and require a lot of energy. The result is often disappointing for all parties involved. It would be more interesting and rewarding to organize a Q&A as a truly curatorial concept, offering insight in sources of inspiration, cherished ambitions and intentions.

*5.5 Researching the International Film Festival Circuit*

Reflection on film festivals was for a long time done exclusively by film critics of newspapers and magazines. The American film critic Kenneth Turan compiled ten of his festival reports in a book: *Sundance to Sarajevo. Film Festivals and the World They Made* (2002). Only recently has a flow of academic publications started to appear. The series of *Film Festival Year Books* published by St. Andrews University Film Studies, for example, started in 2009 and provides thematically-connected overviews of current research. In 2010 the second inventory was still dominated by a search for directions:

> There is no consensus on where the study of film festivals belongs disciplinarily. We tend to place it within film and media studies, yet the existing scholarship is still extremely limited. There is very little in the realm of sociology related to the study of film festivals (and it is usually focused on studying audience demographics); there is little in political science or international relations, little in the study of cultural policy and cultural diplomacy, and there is little in the realm of business and management studies or anthropology. (Iordanova & Cheung 2010: 3)

Film scholar Marijke de Valck is one of the pioneers in the new field of Film Festival Studies. She compiled in cooperation with researcher Skadi Loist an extensive thematic bibliography, published on the website film-festivalresearch.com (Loist and De Valck 2010). This is connected to the *Film Festival Research Network* (FFRN), linked to the *European Network for Cinema and Media Studies* (NECSinitiative.org).

In her study *Film Festivals: From European Geopolitics to Global Cinephilia* (2007), De Valck researched the development and characteristics of the international film festival circuit. She starts with a rough sketch of the historic origins of the European film festivals, which began as a principally glamorous society event, like Venice since 1932 and Cannes since 1946. Film festivals gradually developed into an influential institution for reputation building and promotion of new releases. De Valck divides her investigation of the institutional network of the international film festivals into four aspects: politics, economy, reputation building and programming. Her survey of the geopolitical context is illustrated by the example of the film festival of Berlin. This festival started in 1951 during the Cold War, in a city that was at that time an isolated Western enclave in communist territory. The Berlin festival functioned clearly as a showcase for Western ideology. The Cannes Film Festival serves as an example in her discussion of the economic transformations in the world cinema market and her description of the gap between cultural criteria and business demands. Cannes is part of the competitive international circuit, but is also a European trade market and has therefore to cope with a complex set of demands. In the following chapter concerned with the value-adding process of reputation building, the Venice festival serves as a case study, using four examples of films shown during the 60th edition in 2003: a 'loser' (*Buongiorno, Notte*), a 'winner' (*The Return*), a 'favourite' (*Lost in Translation*) and a 'scandal' (*Twentynine Palms*). In essence, each film festival is a media event, with a specific process of agenda-setting and exposure. It is therefore self-evident that a film festival aims at the creation of as much 'buzz' as possible. The press coverage is dominated by the glamour of film stars on the red carpet and limited to just a handful of sensational world premieres in the festival competition. De Valck concludes her overview taking the International Film Festival Rotterdam as an example of a festival distinguished by an outspoken visionary programming and a 'cinephiliac' audience. Any respectable film festival has also an artistic credo, visible in a clearly profiled choice of films. The research of De Valck provides a clearly defined start for further investigation and research into the phenomenon of film festivals as an institution for the consecration of film art, a trade fair of the film industry and an international exhibition network. The challenge for all of us is to apply her approach to the research of the history of a film festival in your neighbourhood. Giacomo Di Foggia (2014) gives an inspiring starting point for such research.

In a later article De Valck (2012) expands on the issue of the core business of each festival curator, in past and present: finding an audience for each programmed film. This activity of matching is difficult to describe and analyse in an exact way, because there are a large variety of objectives. 'A central problem is the heterogeneity of the film festival circuit: there are many different festivals, with diverging aims and resources, and consequently also many different programming practices' (2012: 26–7).

To get a grip on this dynamic practice of different possible perspectives on programming she uses a periodisation of film festival history, which she already sketched in her earlier study. The first phase consists of three start-up decades (1932–1968), characterised by the presentation of national cinemas selected without curating as we know it today. The second phase is the advent of the 'age of programmers' in the 1970s and 1980s, shifting to advocate art cinema, auteur cinema and discover 'new waves', which are selected on basis of criteria such as 'innovation, originality and topicality'. The programming model of the film festival of Pesaro, founded in 1965, is taken as the blueprint to describe these curatorial changes and developments. The third phase, of 'institutionalisation', started in the 1980s, in which period film festivals attracted new audiences and expanded their practices to offering platforms for support for the film industry. A new genre of 'festival films' was created.

> Programming models became self referential, responding to what people had come to expect of festivals and keeping the system, which legitimised their social function, up and running. (2012: 33)

American researcher and curator Roya Rastegar described in an article in *Screen* her view on the 'curatorial crisis of film festivals', caused by the increased flow of submitted films:

> As digital technologies have provided greater access to the means of film and media productions for those historically disenfranchised from the process, thousands more films are being made each year than can be catalogued or archived. This increase has created a crisis in curating – an urgent need to filter through these productions and connect films with audiences. (2012: 310)

In order to be able to analyse the principles of curatorship of film festivals, Rastegar became a curator herself. In the same article she gives an indication of the constraints of researching the curatorial practice of film festivals:

Researching the highly subjective practices of film curating and festival organizing, however, presents a number of challenges. I first
began my investigation into curatorial work through interviews,
with questions designed to unearth the unspoken negotiations
involved in the process of film selection and audience interpella-
tion. But responses from programmers were akin to the generic,
pre-scripted press releases that reiterate the festival's commitment
to showcase the best, most original or relevant films of the year. I
have since learned that programming is narrated very differently
from how it is practised. The compromises and considerations
required during the selection process are tightly guarded within
the space of the programming room. (2012: 314)

In his column in the Dutch monthly magazine *De Filmkrant* Australian film
critic and researcher Adrian Martin reminisces about his experiences as a
junior staff member of the Melbourne International Film Festival and comments on the difficulties of analysing the phenomenon of film festivals:

Surprisingly, given that film festivals have been such a central part of
cinema culture around the world for so long, there has been alarm-
ingly little study of how they function as complex, social institutions
— not just as showcases for this or that bunch of films, which is how
they are almost always reviewed by critics. (2014)

Researching the curatorship of film festivals needs a systematic approach
to a series of case studies, preferably analysed with compatible methods.
The first step would be to make an inventory of historic and existing ideals
and ambitions of curators: which criteria were used in the past and which
criteria are currently applied? Subsequently we have to describe the results
in a second inventory: which films were selected, rejected, ignored? We
inevitably have to analyse and evaluate the curatorial procedures, to make
a third inventory distinguishing the many restrictions and limitations that
influence the results. The most difficult part is to trace these contextual
influences and formulate them in exact, measurable terms. An extensive
empirical research of patterns and practice of curating film festivals still
remains a challenge. Progress in this field is slow but steady. For an overview see Loist and De Valck (2010) and Hing-Yuk Wong (2011).

An interesting option is to explore the connection between curating film festivals and film archives: many film archives also present a selection of new films, for example the festival L'age d'or started in 1973 by the Royal Film Archive in Brussels. And many film festivals present a side programme of film heritage, for example the series of 'Cannes Classics', started in 2004. The next chapter investigates the world of film archives.

# 6    CURATING FILM ARCHIVES

A film curator can choose to screen newly-made films or earlier works from the film repertoire; in both cases the films in mind are usually still in circulation through the channels of film distribution. A third option is to focus on screening film heritage. But what corpus of film heritage can a cinema curator choose to screen? This depends on what is generally accepted as belonging to film heritage and it is also limited to what parts of film heritage are still available. Film archives play a decisive role in both cases.

## 6.1 The Definition of Film Heritage

The label of 'cultural heritage' includes the subset of 'audiovisual heritage', the designation for the conservation of television material, video material, photographs and movies. 'Film heritage' is a subset within this domain of audiovisual heritage, denoting all available film material. The term 'film' is understood in the broadest sense here, with possible subdivisions such as film art, amateur films, commissioned films, educational films, newsreels and commercials. It is also possible to take the meaning of film heritage even further to include all the material assets within film culture, such as projection devices, cinema interiors, film magazines, movie pictures and movie posters and other film-related archival material. For the sake of clarity here we limit the definition of film heritage to the film material itself. Film heritage could be defined simply as 'all films made more than five to seven years ago'. Film starts in most cases as a consumer good. After five to seven years the first contract for the screening rights expires and then the economic value of the film is determined again. The question is then raised if the film remains in circulation on the market or does it change into a cultural good? Film heritage, then, considered in this way can be viewed as the set of all films made from 1895 to about 2008 (taking 2015 as point of view).

This simple definition of film heritage seems clear but there are some problems to signal. Here is a brief summary of four reservations. First, we need to make a distinction between the films that have been preserved and the films that have gone for good. A significant percentage of film heritage is lost by irretrievable decay or neglect, especially from the period of early cinema. We could name this category of disappeared film heritage 'phantom cinema'. Secondly, there is a large amount of film heritage that still exists but is threatened by deterioration. Film archives worldwide are ringing the alarm bell that their vaults are full of film heritage that is about to perish, or is seriously affected by damages of decay. A complete and sustainable preservation of film heritage is therefore a matter of high urgency, as we will discuss. Thirdly, a large part of film heritage is not available for public screenings in cinemas due to copyright limitations (see also section 3.2). A film archive is allowed to screen a print only if the rights are cleared. It is possible that a perfectly preserved print remains on the shelf if there is no budget for settling the screening permissions and making a distribution print. Fourth and last, one can discuss the criteria for the definition of film heritage, because classifications always have a degree of subjectivity. The phrase 'all movies' raises questions about, for instance, the exact distinction between professional and amateur films. Another discussion would be about the demarcation of the border between film heritage on the one hand and the large amount of surviving electronic and digital images on the other hand.

This leads us into the domain of the ontology of the medium and confronts us with the eternally existing, frequently puzzling question: What is cinema? There are three discussions to be identified on the delimitation of film heritage. The first option is to consider the body of film heritage as a closed entity, defending the thesis that 'cinema is dead'. The second option is to push the boundaries of the whole corpus, labelled as 'expanded cinema'. The third option is to change the classification of the corpus, in other words pushing the boundaries of the canon. Here is a brief elaboration of these three possibilities.

*Cinema is dead*

There is a long tradition of pessimism about the future of film, both as a medium and as art form. The idea of 'the end of cinema' is very old: it always pops up when there are major shifts in technology, such as the advent of sound in 1927, or the emergence of such competitive media as television in the 1950s. At the celebration of the centennial of cinema in 1995, Susan Sontag published a polemic column in which she stated that 'Cinema seems … to be a decadent art' (1996: 60). According to her gloomy vision, idiosyncratic filmmakers no longer get any chance to express themselves freely, while the subculture of cinephilia has disappeared. She observes that film history started with an audience that marveled about the magic of moving images. At a later stage the visit to a cinema became an aesthetic experience, an avid immersion to the image and sound. Sontag observes that after one hundred years we have lost this ability of naive wonder that the first cinema audiences had, and also we lack the cultivated ecstasy of their successors. She points out that the movie experience nowadays is disconnected to the ritual visit of a screening room and also that the corresponding passionate conversation among cinephiles has died. Instead, moving images have become one of the options in home entertainment available to us at will. According to Sontag, a new kind of cinephilia is needed. Also film directors like Peter Greenaway and Jean-Luc Godard belong to the party of critics, moaning the loss of the true cinema experience. The pessimistic-nostalgic view of the demise of film art was continued by, among others, the American film critic Godfrey Cheshire (1998). Film researcher Stefan Jovanovic (2003) offers an inventory of several 'downfall' thoughts which had appeared in several publications. One year later the Australian online magazine *Senses of Cinema* made a survey among experts about the future of cinema, which resulted in a series of gloomy testimonials (see Erickson 2004). Researcher Deb Verhoeven (2013) has offered the most recent reflection on the issue of the status of film. For curators of film archives it is less common to make an argument about the end of cinema. They are confronted in their research with the paradoxical situation that the available collection that could be used to be incorporated in their programmes is both very incomplete and at the same time still too large to overlook. Even if the cinema should really be considered dead, then there remains sufficient material for fascinating archival film programmes.

## Expanded cinema

In former days, the medium of film was strictly bound to a theatrical release, in other words a projection in a cinema characterised by a linear laps of time, a collective viewing experience and an intangible fleeting image stream. Since the event of video and DVD and now streaming, there is the possibility of showing films in private spaces, characterised by an individual personalised viewing experience, with opportunities for repetition, stops and selections. The monopoly of the cinema for exhibiting films is over. The technical development in the field of distribution has implications for the screening situation, both from an artistic and a business perspective. The cinema sells itself as the only place where the medium of film can be fully enjoyed, because of the big screen, the immersive sound, the comfortable seats. The cinema is the only place where film art can be seen in its original state, as a closed unit with a continuous, linear display in a darkened room and a committed audience (not distracted by popcorn, soda drinks or mobile phones). This option of authenticity, however, has got competition from several respectable alternatives such as multiple screen installations, interactive exhibits of monitors, urban screens and other site-specific cinema (for instance the project *Sleepwalkers*, created by artist Doug Aitken in 2007 on the facade of the Museum of Modern Art in New York). The most extreme boundary shifts are visible in the contemporary avant-garde film, a small subset of the total film heritage. The term 'expanded cinema' is used to indicate works that stretch the boundaries of the medium (see also section 7.2). It is not a very new phenomenon; the term is derived from the title of the book by Gene Youngblood in 1970 about the American avant-garde artists in the 1960s; see also Marchessault and Lord (2008) and Uroskie (2014).

## An expanded film canon

Film heritage traditionally contains a small set of 'canonic films' (see also section 3.3), but in addition to this, a still growing number of film historiographic studies have given attention to previously ignored aspects of film heritage. A clear example is the historical focus on the period of early cinema (roughly 1895–1920). Also the attention on what were considered to be peripheral areas of the corpus increased. The category of these so-called 'ephemeral films' may include corporate films, advertising films, newsreels, educational films, amateur films (home movies) or unused film recordings (deleted scenes, outtakes). Besides this relatively new category more established designations exist, such as 'cult films, 'camp', 'trash films' and 'underground cinema'. There are many works which were initially seen as niche areas of the film spectrum ('fringe cinema'), but now have their own canonical development and are increasingly recognised as special areas of film production, alongside such designations as 'mainstream entertainment' and 'independent art film'. Canonical cult films for example are *Who Are You, Polly Maggoo* (William Klein, 1966), *Barbarella* (Roger Vadim, 1968), *The Rocky Horror Picture Show* (Jim Sharman, 1975) and *Priscilla, Queen of the Desert* (Stephen Elliott, 1994). John Waters positioned himself most clearly as an intentional camp director with films as *Hairspray* (1988) and *Cry Baby* (1990). The term 'cult films' refers to movies or TV shows that are appreciated by a small group of fanatical admirers, the essence of the pleasure lying in a largely unreasoned enthusiasm, a collective ecstatic viewing experience with a select group of sympathisers. 'Camp' is about an unruly, rebellious fascination for movies or TV shows that do not meet the requirements of traditional aesthetics. Camp movies and TV series are so ugly that they become pretty hilarious. They are old-fashioned in a superlative way, offering simple and schematic stories, highly artificial and unrealistic settings, or a combination of all of these qualifications at the same time. Cult and camp are designations which are located close to each other. In both cases, the viewer is subversive in his appreciation: ugliness and unnaturalness serve as a recommendation. The audiences are part of a subculture; they appreciate what is deliberately suppressed or denied by the mainstream culture. Spectators form a closed group with its own code. The aesthetic judgement takes the form of an ironic pose, a decadent extravagance, a sublimation of triviality, or simply a sign of idiosyncratic taste and indulgence. The audience play a decisive role in the reception of films. *The Sound of Music* (Robert Wise, 1965), for instance, was an enormous success on release, a popular mainstream romantic musical film that decades later became a cult classic. The Gay and Lesbian Film Festival in London 1988 marked the beginning of the craze for special screenings characterised by intensive audience participation, with spectators who dress in appropriate costumes and respond with collective singalongs and use of accessories (including flashlights). More examples are discussed in Jankovich *et al* (2003) and Telotte (1991).

*6.2 Preserving and Presenting Film Heritage*

Film heritage is a relatively clearly delimited corpus in the art world, firstly because films were made only from 1895 and secondly because many films, especially from the silent period, have been lost in the course of time. In a recent blogpost, David Bordwell explained the situation of scarcity:

> Until very recently, the commercial market place couldn't be counted on to preserve films adequately. Because films were circulated and shown in a rapid rhythm, and because they were regarded as ephemeral entertainments, very few production firms maintained libraries of their output. Gaumont of France and Nordisk of Denmark are rare examples of companies who saw the virtue of storing their films, and even those collections were not complete. The American companies often destroyed their back catalogues in order to save space and money. As a result, only a tiny percentage of the world's silent film output survives today. (2014b)

In September 2013 the US Library of Congress commissioned film historian and archivist David Pierce to do an inventory of the remaining films of the American studios in the period 1912–1919. His conclusion was that 70 per cent of these films no longer exist (2013). A similar quota applies for European films in this period. The global film heritage from the early days is quite a melted iceberg; all the more reason to cherish what we do have at our disposal. We could specify the act of 'cherishing' as three fundamental tasks of film archives. Firstly, the safeguarding of the collection: to acquire, minimising the loss of value and restore if necessary the films to their original form. Secondly, the presentation of the collection: offering as much as possible in the way of screenings, exhibitions, publications. Thirdly, the development of the collection: adding value, giving it a connection to current times and contexts.

*Task 1: The safeguarding of the collection*

The need to safeguard film heritage can be translated into three subtasks of the film archive: collection assembling, preservation and restoration.

1a. Collection assembling – What strategy has the film archive in terms of collection assembling? What criteria are formulated for the selection of potential acquisitions and how effective is this? What criteria does one possibly need for disposal of the collection? We could identify a pro-active 'shaping approach' in which the collection serves to safeguard the versatility of the collective memory, and a more passive 'reflecting approach' in which the collection tries to give a representative section of several past and present film cultures. In practice, the strategy of a film archive will combine both approaches.

Most of the acquisitions of a film archive are derived from the catalogues of film distributors. A film print (footage or files) have initially economic status; they are part of a series of identical copies intended for international circulation within the system of commercial exploitation. Once a film print arrives at the film archive, however, it is given the status of an authentic object, part of the collection of film heritage.

It is an empirical fact that the sale of even rare examples of twentieth-century cinema yield little money, there is not a thriving auction market. Film archives are not used to paying for the acquisition of private collections, because their investment consists of the process of preservation and making the film accessible. Another important source of acquisitions are the donations of collections of private collectors and filmmakers. EYE Film Insitute Netherlands, for example, acquired the last existing print of the silent film *Beyond the Rocks* (Sam Woods, 1922) from the estate of a Dutch private collector for free, but spent half a million Euros in 2005 on the digital restoration of this sensational recovered silent treasure.

Assembling a film collection means inevitably to be confronted with the practical problem of a very diverse practice of 'legal deposit' in the international film industry. There is no general rule or law concerning the mandatory donations of an undamaged and complete print of each film that is brought into circulation. Legal deposit is a key moment in the final phase of film production, but simultaneously, it is also the first phase of film preservation. When the final cut is finished, a master print of every film should be donated automatically to a film archive, to guarantee that a print of the most pristine quality of both image and sound is to be preserved, as a possible source for reference and distribution in the future. This ideal could be reached by a mandatory deposit of films, as is the case in countries like France, Italy, Norway, Finland and Denmark. However, in many countries, there is only a voluntary deposit. Gorini observes an ideological choice in this area of cultural policy:

> The choice is essentially between exhaustiveness and selection. At one end lies the view, which is best represented in the French approach, that all films deserve to be preserved irrespective of their nature, quality and commercial success because each constitutes a unique element of the country's historical and cinematographic memory. At the other end is the belief that collecting and preserving all works is neither feasible nor desirable and that the only sensible option is to take a selective approach. (2004: 4)

1b. Preservation – The film print has long been a physical object in the shape of a film strip, distributed in rolls in film cans. Up to the 1950s nitrate was used as the image carrier but it proved to be inept because it is a highly inflamable material and pulverises in the long run. Although there are many stories to tell about presumed lost films that are saved just in time, far too many nitrate films have already been irretrievably lost. The films on the more sustainable image carrier of celluloid (acetate or polyester) also have a clear expiration date: after some decades the colours fade (this is called the 'vinegar syndrome'). There is a need for massive preservation of all these film prints, but this is very costly and time consuming.

The twenty-first century has brought a shift towards 'born digital material', elusive computer files in the form of bit streams. Digital technology is relatively new and still developing fast, therefore the durability of digital files remains uncertain and there is also the issue of compatibility or interoperability. It is also still uncertain which format will become the future standard. Digital storage systems are quickly outdated and require regular upgrading. Constant migration and backing up of files is also necessary.

Film archives are debating the options for the best long-term preservation strategy, aiming for the highest grade of sustainability and safety of data storage and access. In the meanwhile, expectations about accessibility to film heritage are increasing. Film archivists are therefore confronted with the existence of critical tensions between raising costs and restricted budgets, facing permanently changing standards and procedures of preservation.

1c. Restoration – The approach to film restoration seems at first glance quite simple: go to work quickly and simply recover all existing damages. But it is less clear than it seems, because there is a range of possible violations of the film during the circulation, with a possible range of errors and modifications. An intertitle in a silent film, for example, may be incorrectly translated, or put in the wrong place or in the wrong order, or added later. Yet the film print in this 'corrupt state' could also be seen as a sign of how the film culture looked like in the past. Cinema is an art form based on the mechanical reproduction of the original. It is possible to duplicate each film print endlessly. However, there are often various versions of a film, due to censorship, business decisions or artistic views. The definition of the 'original' in cinema art is therefore problematic. The pressing question is: which version do you present? The most evident choice would be to consider the master print of the version which was shown at the world premiere as the original, but there remain artistic and material choices. For instance: what about a 'director's cut' made several years later? And is a 70mm celluloid print of *Play Time* (Jacques Tati, 1967) more 'authentic' than a 35mm celluloid print, or a digital file (DCP)? There are several equally respectable opinions about the best way to implement 'improvements' and also different views on the concept of 'authenticity ' and 'restoring the original'. A film archive will have to find a balance between the conflicting demands of respect for the authenticity of the work, the documentation value of the surviving film and the free accessibility for a contemporary audience.

*Task 2: The presentation of the collection*

The ideal film archive provides a broad overview of the whole of film history and establishes a link between the film culture in the past and present, both with films from the collection and with movies from other sources. The presentation of the collection can be done through creating a carefully curated programme, both in house and touring nationally, put into context by offering a fringe programme of reflection and information, with exhibitions, debates, lectures, publications, educational meetings. Besides that, the collection should be made accessible by constructing a distribution catalogue and a video-on-demand platform. However, between dream and reality there are many obstacles. One of them is clearance of the screening rights (see section 3.2). Another practical constraint is the availability of the film print. In this area there was a long struggle in the archival world. In the view of archival pioneers such as Ernest Lindgren in the UK, or Jan de Vaal in the Netherlands, films from their archives could only be screened if there was a distribution print available. All unique prints remain on the shelf, because it is irresponsible to risk damage. In contrast, other archival pioneers such as Henri Langlois in France or Jacques Ledoux in Belgium held the conviction that any archival film should be shown, because that is the ultimate purpose of a film archive. For an overview of this discussion see also Cherchi Usai (2000).

Curating film heritage contains a special category: the silent film. The films from the period 1895–1927 have no spoken dialogue or direct sound. For a twenty-first century audience silent film is a separate art form. Silent film requires a mental adjustment for the current viewer, a habituation to the imagery of the past. The showing of silent films is usually done with a musical accompaniment, whether or not 'live'. The fundamental question is: what music do we add to silent movies? It could be a reconstruction of the original score if this has been preserved, or using original cue sheets, or involve commissioning a new musical improvisation, or a new composition, or opting for a collage of existing compositions (see also section 7.1). A film curator in a film archive could choose to present his silent film programme outside the comfort zone of the screening room. A conventional take on this option is to organise, for example, live musical accompaniments of silent films with full orchestra in a huge concert hall. The London Film Festival has an impressive track record in this area. Several specialised 'archive film festivals' offer additional options (see Marlow-Mann 2013 and Di Chiara and Re 2011). Another strategy is to choose more unconventional possibilities for pop-up cinema screenings. The genre of Gothic films, for instance, has many great silent classics such as *The Fall of the House of*

*Usher* (Jean Epstein, 1928). It would be a spooky experience to present this film for a very selective audience in the setting of a deserted mansion together with a live performance of an appropiate score or improvisation. The spell of the haunted castle would burst from the screen!

*Task 3: The development of the collection*

The question of where we can locate and position film heritage is still relevant. Most of the film heritage was originally created for screenings in the cinema, but this dominance of the public domain is over. Film heritage has become a hybrid phenomenon. It is both a projection of a light beam as well as a computer file. It still can be presented through the traditional 'apparatus' of the projection in a movie theatre, but it is also available in the private domain in an individual multimedia environment. Film heritage has an ambiguous status: Is it a remnant of a glorious past and are we therefore dealing with a mummified art form? Or is it a historical medium that is revitalised by new media? Inevitably, we are once again confronted with the fundamental ontological question: What is cinema?

Each screening has the historical context of a public that was then and there fascinated by the moving images. We can look back on a long series of individual viewing experiences in a public space. The network of film archives preserves the remains of this more than a hundred years of presentation practice. Besides films, the archive collection also includes film-related objects, such as posters, devices, documents and comments. What value have these objects for society at large, or for specific individuals? We can distinguish five possible values of film heritage. Firstly, historical value, meaning safeguarding historical stories about national identity, documenting historical artistic quality. Secondly, connecting value, expressed by advancing interaction between different generations, subcultures, social groups. Thirdly, educational value, implying potential of learning and exploring in an informal way. Fourthly, entertainment value, resulting in experiencing unusual events. And last but not least economic value, realised by re-use by the creative industry.

*Conclusion*

There are many stories to tell about films that have been saved from oblivion, and about the archivists who rescued essential film heritage. The task for the film curator is to present all avaible treasures in an attractive way to an audience. One option is to create a 'Silent Season' or a series of 'Cinema Classics', to build up an audience and to promote loyalty. Another option is to create a big event, a once in a lifetime experience, setting up a festival ambience and creating momentum. A good example of this is to be found in the restoration and presentation of *Napoléon* (Abel Gance, 1927), which had a successful world tour and screened in several huge concert halls twice already (see Brownlow 2004). Another example is to be found in the recent exhibition *Jean Desmet's Dream Factory: The Adventurous Years of Film (1907–1916)* at the EYE Film Institute Netherlands in 2015, offering an overview of decades of archival work: safeguarding, presenting and developing a specific collection acquired as a legacy of a distribution company. More details about the exhibition policy of EYE Film Institute are given in section 7.2.

Not everybody is convinced yet of the value of film heritage. Besides many films known to be lost we have to admit that there are even more forgotten films, disappeared into oblivion. Seen from the perspective of the insiders, all seems clear enough: film heritage is important, valuable, indispensable. And all parts of film heritage are potentially inspirational, intriguing and fascinating. The most urgent question is how we can convey this opinion to a general public and to cultural policymakers. How can we ameliorate the awareness of film heritage in an attractive and lasting way? The next chapter contains two case studies dealing with this question: the challenge to programme silent feature films succesfully and the options to curate cinema exhibitions in an innovative way.

# 7    CASE STUDIES

*7.1 Programming Silent Feature Films: People on Sunday (1930)*

Curating programmes of silent films implies a special task and challenge. The body of work concerned exists of films made in the period between 1895 and roughly 1927, so this raises the question of what kind of relation these very old films could hold for an audience in the twenty-first century (see also Withall 2014). It is certainly necessary to bridge the gap of underevaluation caused by prejudices. Granted, there is a sliding scale of quality to acknowledge. Some films need to be seen in their historical context in order to be able to enjoy them; indeed, they require an effort to understand them. The task of the film curator is to do just this: discover the quality that is not immediatly obvious and recognisable. But on the other hand the spectrum of silent films also contains many impressive masterpieces that withstand the test of time gloriously and can be enjoyed autonomously, and yet they are still not widely known. It is one of the priviliges of a film curator to highlight these masterpieces of the early cinema. In my view, *Menschen am Sonntag (People on Sunday)* deserves to be screened regularly and frequently because it is an extraordinary silent film, with a timeless appeal. This case study elaborates on formulating arguments to support this statement. But first a few practical issues should be noted.

*Providing a score for People on Sunday*

Screening silent films also entails the inevitable necessity of thinking about adding appropiate music. Happily enough, there is a rich choice of options. In the case of *People on Sunday* there are various audio tracks available on the BluRay disc (region 1) and several other DVD editions, but at a screening it is more rewarding to arrange for a live accompaniment because this results in a totally different viewing experience. The musicians give the audience their personal musical interpretations of the film and there will be a subtle resonance between audience and performers, and beween the old film and the new music. Especially with improvising musicians there is a positive tension of unsuspected twists and unpredictable moods. Live music is a kiss of life for silent films; see also Loiperdinger (2011).

What are the options for providing a score in the case of *People on Sunday*? The most historically accurate approach would be to choose for a reconstruction of the original score played at the premiere in 1930. This score was compiled by Otto Stenzel who arranged several tunes from Czech composers into a medley. However, there is a lack of exact documentation, meaning a reconstruction remains problematic. A commonly used alternative is to ask a pianist to provide an improvisation. This practice has resulted in a wide range of professionals who offer high quality solo interpretations. Regarding *People on Sunday* there is evidence of acclaimed performances by Donald Sosin (US), Neil Brand (UK), Darius Battiwalla (UK), Martin Rohrmeier (Germany), Stephan von Bothmer (Germany), Wilfried Kaets (Germany), Hilde Nash (Belgium) and Wim van Tuyl (the Netherlands). Dutch pianist Wim van Tuyl chose another approach in 1999, selecting an informed medley of music taken from a historical collection of 78rpm gramophone discs.

Several scores were registrated on DVD. In 2000, Australian composer Elena Kats-Chemin made an orchestral score, commisioned by broadcast companies ZDF/Arte. In 2005 German percussionist Steven Garling made his score for *People on Sunday*. At the Rimusicazioni Film Festival in Bolzano four different scores were presented in 2008 and subsequently released on DVD. In the United States the Mont Alto Orchestra presented their score in 2009 and recorded it two years later for the Criterion release. On the Internet there are many traces to be found of other musical interpretations of *People on Sunday*. In 2002 the German Trio Bravo+ performed their score at the 'Jewish Culture Days' in Berlin. In 2003 another trio of German musicians made a tour of nine cinemas with their version, featuring Nils Rohwer (vibraphone & marimba), Jens Schliecker (piano) and Jens Tolksdorf (saxophone). More recently the German DJ Raphaël Marionneau and DJ D'dread each made a score, which they both performed live in 2013. The Alliage Orchestra, an occasional ensemble of Dutch composers and musicians, revived at the International Documentary Film Festival Amsterdam (IDFA) 2014 their score made in 2000 consisting of a soundscape of electronic loops and grooves, samples and additional acoustically played music. The most recent score is composed by Albert van Veenendaal, for a trio of altviolin, harp and prepared piano (February 2014 at the EYE Film Institute Netherlands, Amsterdam).

*Preservation and restoration of People on Sunday*

All these different approaches to musical interpretation were possible because in the 1990s *People on Sunday* was carefully restored. The best preserved print, surprisingly enough, proved to be available in Amsterdam. *People on Sunday* was released in the Netherlands in November 1930 by the film club distributor Centraal Bureau Ligafilms and shown in Dutch film clubs in Rotterdam, Utrecht, Arnhem and later also in Amsterdam (in the cinema De Uitkijk, which still exists). This distribution 35mm print was stored safely through the years and ended up in the archive of the Dutch Filmmuseum (now EYE Film Institute Netherlands). In 1930, the intertitles of *People on Sunday* were translated into Dutch and also adapted into a minimalistic, modernist typography because this was the 'corporate style' of the avant-garde film club. The restoration included, among other elements, a return to the original German intertitles. During the restoration project all available versions were carefully compared and combined, yet there are seven or eight minutes of the original film that remain missing (circa 175 metres of celluloid). Martin Koerber (2000) offers a detailed report of the restoration. In 2014 a digital scan of the 35mm projection print was made and most of the scratches and other damages were cleaned up digitally.

*How to promote People on Sunday*

The task of a film curator in a film archive is to cherish the existence of all preserved films. The first step is to provide for a pristine print, but this alone is not sufficient. It is also necessary to show them to an as large audience as possible. If one was to schedule *People on Sunday* without sufficient notice or elaboration, one would probably end up with just a few visitors. So, how to convince potential target groups about how exciting and enjoyable these old films are? How to argue that silent films in particular present gripping stories and fascinating views, still perfectly recognisable to today's viewers? Inspiration could be found in the overview of possible arguments for a critical value judgement in section 3.3. A second source of inspiration is the website of the DVD label Criterion, which includes a set of promotion trailers for each of their releases. These trailers have a uniform format of enumerating three solid reasons why one might appreciate the movie in question. In the case of *People on Sunday* the three arguments are formulated as 'The Timelessness of "Twenty-somethings"', 'Beautiful Berlin Before the War' and 'The Youthful Talent of Five Future Hollywood Masters' (see criterion.com). In an additional essay, commissioned by Criterion, film critic Noah Isenberg describes *People on Sunday* thus:

> The style of the film is natural, the setting unpretentious, and the atmosphere, perhaps the core of the project, shamelessly flirtatious. More than anything else, a new kind of directness, an unmediated, unvarnished representation of everyday life as experienced by members of a young, urban consumer class, is what the filmmakers seem to have been after, in defiant contrast to the spectacular big-budget pictures being produced by UFA at the time.

For a persuasive exposition of the unique quality and relevance of *People on Sunday* it is possible to expand on this.

*Argument 1: The sparkling youth*

In the summer of 1929, a group of ambitious young friends decided to make a realistic fiction film about a summer Sunday in Berlin. Their starting point for the project was the simple question: what do ordinary young people do on their day off? The answer was straightforward: on Sundays young people just enjoy their free time. To demonstrate this, two young men and three young women were chosen to pose as representatives of their generation. They act out how a typical Saturday night and Sunday might be for their generation. We see them taking the S-Bahn to the woods and beaches of the Nicholas See (Lake Nicholas). They chat and flirt and listen to music. As members of modern youth, they take a portable gramophone with them. The song 'In einer kleinen Konditorei' is presented as example of a popular tune of that time.

The result of shooting on weekends looks like a creative documentary. Through the eye of the camera we are given a comprehensive and relaxed portrait of daily life of the time. *People on Sunday* offers journalistic and humorous observations on the social codes of urban leisure time and street life. Every scene is recorded on location, for the most part in the open air. There is time taken for some asides: we follow the protagonists on their day trip, but also get extended glimpses of anonymous citizens. The result is an almost documentary representation of family recreation at the city beaches, with sunny bathing scenes contrasting with images of busy traffic and crowded public transport. Berlin was a large, vibrant city, and in 1929 life in Germany was still carefree. Following the footsteps of five easy-going young people having a good time, we get a clear and realistic view of the tolerant and relaxed atmosphere of this metropolis.

The opening sequence sets the mood. The film starts with a dynamic sequence of observations of city life, some skillful editing of moving trains, automobiles and pedestrians. The five protagonists are introduced through short vignettes. Two of them subtly emerge from the background of the traffic, they are initially shown without attracting special attention but are gradually highlighted. We see a road crossing near the Bahnhof Zoo subway station. The camera is placed high above the scene, offering a high-angle view, not dissimilar to a modern-day surveillance camera. We watch from a distance what is happening on the street. A young woman is waiting, a young man saunters around her. It looks like an educational film about a predator circling around his prey. How will the male convince the female to join him for a date? We see how he takes his time, addresses her finally, but we are too far away to hear anything. Apparently, he is a smooth talker, because in the blink of an eye they are sitting together at a nearby café terrace, eating ice creams. The camera has advanced close by, sitting next to them low on the ground, offering us a clear view of their animated conversation. Naturally – it is a silent film – we still do not hear anything, but it soon becomes clear that she accepts a date for the next day, the famous Sunday. It is agreed that she takes a girl friend with her and he also is accompanied by a friend.

The process of dating and flirting in 1929 very much resembles the same activities in our times. The party on Sunday consists of the charming young man and his robust friend, whose girlfriend stays at home sleeping the whole day. The two remaining young women are competing for the attention of the only free man in the group. Their rivalry becomes more sharp-tongued along the day, but the summer is too sunny for dark jealousy to blossom. The blonde girl seems to fall into an amorous enchantment. There is even a clear hint of casual sex in the woods, but this passion flows away as easily as it manifests itself. In the glowing afternoon they decide to hire a pedalo. The two young gentlemen are showing off, playing around. Their attention is attracted by two other ladies in a rowing boat, who are pretending to be helpless damsels in distress, and very happy indeed to be rescued.

The story of the bashful romance has an open ending. The blonde girl and the charming young man promise to meet each other the following Sunday, but we know that it is very uncertain how this will turn out. To start with, when the girl is out of sight the men express their preference to attend a soccer match next week. It is a timeless truth: sports are the main rival in many love stories. The film closes with images of the empty streets, early Monday morning, soon filling with all the citizens of the big city who are starting their day of work. The graphic intertitles cry out: it is Monday again! The new working week starts with a strong and enormous longing for the next Sunday.

*Argument 2: Berlin, Berlin*

There are often moments where silent movies leave the spectators with a bittersweet feeling of nostalgia for the past, showing the details of daily life in bygone times. *People on Sunday* is a film which offers a series of these moments. Naturally, it is impossible for us to enter physically the year 1929, but for an instant we are able to cherish the thought that we could have been present there and then and that it would have been possible for us to mingle in the crowd. What a delight it would have been to wander around the town and observe the people!

However, it would be inevitable that our peception during this walk would be influenced by our knowledge of the historical events in Germany after 1929. In the film there is, for instance, a sequence on the beach, with a photographer taking portraits of passersby (and some friends of the film team, such as actress/dancer Valeska Gert). It is a fascinating depiction of different behaviour before a camera: laughing, smiling and posing. Each take wonderfully halts in a freeze frame on the faces of a man, woman or child. This is a heartwarming scene, but today we inevitably notice that there are many Jewish faces among them. Their carefree holiday spirit betrays a dark shadow to us, because we know that it is very likely that within fifteen years these same people will either be murdered or forced to flee the country, as the mostly Jewish film crew indeed did. Some outdoor scenes were shot at the Wann See, at that time this was just another city beach. The infamous 'Wann See Conference' was still far ahead. Another historical landmark is the Brandenburg Gate. In the film there is only a glimpse of this imperial arch, as a detail in a montage sequence, but this monument has now become first and foremost a historically charged icon of Nazism. Another small detail in the film is the group of marching soldiers. In 1927 this was maybe an innocent activity, but we cannot help but notice that the public on both sides of the street react with such enthusiasm that it might make us uncomfortable as they appear totally absorbed by this sight, applauding without restraint. All these details disturb our sweet feelings of nostalgia. Still, the film will have a special resonance for everyone who visits Berlin and it would be fascinating to try to revisit the locations of the film and to duplicate the Sunday outing. This, however, would not be easy, because contemporary Berlin has changed beyond recognition, partly due to certain, well-known, historical events but also because of the general change in city development that arose later in the twentieth century. Even the iconic trains of the S-Bahn have been modernised. And also the station kiosk with a wide assortment of services and products, such as a public telephone, a collection of audacious postcards, and glasses of fresh milk or 'schorle morle' (wine mixed with mineral water), has vanished.

*Argument 3: A talented team*

Everybody behind the camera was young, and nearly all were to become famous later on. The ultra-low-budget film was made as a collective effort by a very talented team of young professionals. Billy Wilder (23 years old in 1929) and Fred Zinnemann (22 years old) were destined to have lengthy successful careers in the film business. As we know this happened in Hollywood because they were forced to leave Germany. The same goes for the brothers Robert Siodmak (aged 29) and Curt Siodmak (aged 27), and Edgar G. Ulmer (aged 25) and also director of photography Eugen Schüfftan (aged 36). An account of their careers is easy to trace in various sources, starting with the Internet Movie Database (IMDb.com) for an inventory of the bare facts. I restrict myself to a very selective summary: Eugen Schüfftan made stopovers in England (*The Robber Symphony*, 1936), the Netherlands (*Komedie om geld*, 1936) and France (*Le quai des brumes*, 1938). He received the Academy Award for Best Cinematography in 1962 for *The Hustler* (black & white, Cinemascope). Edgar G. Ulmer acquired fame with low-budget films such as the film noir *Detour* (1945). Curt Siodmak became a slightly embittered scriptwriter for many B-movies. His brother Robert Siodmak acquired fame as director of film noirs such as *Phantom Lady* (1944), *The Killers* (1946) and *Criss Cross* (1949). Fred Zinnemann became a mainstream director of big-budget productions like *From Here to Eternity* (1953). And Billy Wilder does not need any introduction.

*People on Sunday* has all the qualities of a very successful graduation film, only there was no film academy or any other formal training in these times. It is a timeless and inspiring example of what is possible if you go outside and follow your ambition and convictions. A group of young people made a film, with help from their amateur friends and together they achieved their mission: to show real life of real people on a summer's day in Berlin. They made the film 'without actors' as the subtitle proclaims. The result is a hybrid film, combining staged reality with a wide range of cinematographic observations. In a gentle way the film makes fun of the star system and the cult of fabulous divas. Indeed, none of the actors in *People on Sunday* were professionals; before their appearance in the film they had no formal training as actors. This is no problem, because in a silent film there is no need for professional diction. It is amazing how graceful and natural they move around, seemingly unaware of the camera. The visual style of the film granted them beautiful close-ups, just like real matinee idols. The camera work is dynamic, with a fluent variation of low and high angles, long shots and close ups. The editing is also well paced and rhythmic. The activities of the protagonists are interspersed with play-ful asides, like the aforementioned sequence of the photographer on the beach, without disrupting the main storyline. There is also a moment of mild satire in the scene ridiculing a proud nationalist sitting on a bench near a monumental statue, but *People on Sunday* shows us mostly a world without shadows.

*People on Sunday* marks the very end of the era of silent film, because the transition to film sound had already started in 1927. It was a good choice not to create a sound track, because the technology was still both primitive and complex, and the story of the big city and its citizens should indeed be told purely visually, without the use of spoken dialogue. The intertitles are used with careful restraint, offering short sections of dialogue in a Berlin dialect. We also witness the well-balanced insert of several breathtaking montage sequences: a series of documentary takes, a free improvisation on the theme of life in the metropolis. *People on Sunday* is recommended to all who are in the mood to experience a moment of relaxed wandering around on a sunny day in Berlin.

*How to program People on Sunday*

It is necessary to keep in mind that silent films are best appreciated the way they were intended to be shown, namely on the big screen with a live musical accompaniment. Any single screening of *People on Sunday* in this mode can be made relevant and attractive for an audience of today. Added value could possibly be found in scheduling a screening at the date of its official world premiere, 4 February 1930. We can look forward to the centennial celebration in 2030, but why not mark earlier anniversaries? Another option is to search for a special location, for instance an open air screening during a summer festival on a city beach anywhere in the world. It is also possible to put the screening of this authentic and inspirational feature film in a broader context, in several ways. Here are a few options for curating a programme around this silent film. This is an addition to the options of criteria for curating a film programme listed in section 4.1.

A first option can be 'curating by location'. The city of Berlin was a source of inspiration for various other Weimar films, for example:

- *Die Stadt der Millionen: Ein Lebensbild Berlins* (Adolf Trotz, 1925, 80').
- *Berlin, die Sinfonie der Grossstadt* (Walter Ruttmann, 1927, 69').

- *Markt in Berlin / Markt am Wittenbergerplatz* (Wilfried Basse, 1929, 20')
- *Jagd auf Dich: Filmdarsteller aus dem Kinopublikum* (Ernst Angel, 1930, 42')
- *Berliner Stilleben* (László Moholy-Nagy, 1931, 9')
- *Berlin Alexanderplatz* (Piel Jutzi, 1931, 90', based on the novel by Alfred Döblin).

A second option can be to choose 'curating by subject', and select additional films based on their engagement with daily life of the lower classes in the Weimar period (1919–1933). From this perspective of content we could start by investigating the corpus of 'Zillefilms', a series of impressionistic films made in the 1920s about the Berlin proletariat. These films contain realistic stories about workers and jobless people in tenement houses, depicting their gloomy existence in crowded living spaces in the 'Hinterhof'. Examples include:

- *Die Verrufenen: Der fünften Stand* (*The Slums of Berlin*, Gerhard Lamprecht 1925).
- *Die Unehelichen* (*Children of No Importance*, Gerhard Lamprecht, 1926).
- *Die Da Unten* (Victor Janson, 1926)
- *Menschen Untereinander* (*People Among Each Other*, Gerhard Lamprecht, 1926)
- *Schwere Jungen – leichte Mädchen* (Carl Boese, 1927)
- *Unter den Laterne* (*Under the Lantern*, Gerhard Lamprecht, 1928).
- *Grossstadtkinder* (*City Children*, Arthur Haase, 1929).

These examples could possibly be compared with other German 'social problem films' such as:

- *Hintertreppe* (*Backstairs*, Leopold Jessner, 1921, starring Henny Porten)
- *Die freudlose Gasse* (*Joyless Street*, G. W. Pabst, 1925, starring Greta Garbo, Asta Nielsen)
- *Die Gesunkenen* (*The Fallen*, Rudolf Walter-Fein and Rudolf Dworsky, 1926, starring Asta Nielsen)
- *So ist das Leben* (Carl Junghaus, 1929, set in Prague)

- *Mutter Krausens fahrt ins Glück* (*Mother Krause's Journey to Happiness*, Piel Jutzi, 1929)
- *Kuhle Wampe, oder: Wem gehört die Welt* (Slatan Dudow, 1932)
- *Die Carmen von St. Pauli* (*Docks of Hamburg*, E. Waschneck, 1928)
- *Jenseits der Strasse* (*Harbor Drift*, L. Mitler 1929)
- *Razzia in St. Pauli* (*Raid in St. Pauli*, W. Hochbaum 1932)

A third option can be 'curating by theme'. At the Berlin International Film Festival of 2007 a sidebar programme titled 'City Girls: Images of Women in Silent Film' was presented, containing *People on Sunday* and 29 other silent films. This is a specific aspect of the representation of the metropolis in 'city symphonies' and other silent films. There is a large corpus of silent movies about the big city, like the famous *Rien que les heures* (*Nothing But Time*, Alberto Cavalcanti, 1926), or *Chelovek s kino-apparatom* (*Man With a Movie Camera*, Dziga Vertov, 1929), but also the fiction film *Piccadilly* (E. A. Dupont, 1929), or the lesser known documentary *Welstadt in Flegeljahren: Ein bericht über Chicago* (Heinrich Hauser, 1931). *People on Sunday* offers an interesting addition to comparable impressions of big cities seen in other avant-garde silent films, such as *Berlin, die Sinfonie der Grossstadt* or the short film *Berliner Stillleben*. In the same period another short avant-garde film was produced in France, also about daily life in the metropolis (in this case Paris) and observering the events in a holiday resort at the bank of the river Marne: *Nogent, eldorado du dimanche* (Marcel Carné, 1929). The silent fiction film *Au bonheur des dames* (Julien Duvivier, 1929) contains a sequence of an outing for the staff of the department store, enjoying themselves at the village L'isle-Adam. And we could think of an American silent movie like *Lonesome* (Paul Fejos, 1928), with sequences of urban recreation at the beaches of Coney Island. A thematic correspondance with *People on Sunday* is also to detect in the German short film *Ins Blaue hinein* (Eugen Schüfftan, 1931), an early sound film. The metropolis is a favorable subject in many other sound films too. A few options are: *La Seine a rencontré Paris* (*The Seine Meets Paris*, Joris Ivens, 1957), *Ya shagayu po Moskve* (*Walking the Streets of Moscow*, Gergiy Daneliya, 1964) or *Any Way the Wind Blows* (Tom Barman, 2003).

A fourth option can be 'curating by association', resulting in, for example, a line up as follows:

- *Bank Holiday* (Carol Reed, 1938)
- *Domenica d'Agosto* (*Sunday in August*, Luciano Emmer, 1950)
- *Mne dvadtsat let* (*I am Twenty*, Marlen Khutsiev, 1965)
- *Sonnabend, Samstag und Montag früh* (Hannes Schönemann, 1978)
- *Du Mich Auch* (*Same to You*, Dani Levy *et al*, 1986)
- *Mein Langsames Leben* (*Passing Summer*, Angela Schanelec, 2001)

These feature films could be screened in combination with shorts such as *Noon Time Activities* (Ernie Gehr, 2004).

Start curating your own programme, or just go to visit the next screening of *People on Sunday*. Hopefully this case study offered enough arguments and inspirations to do so.

*7.2 Curating Cinema Exhibitions – 'Found Footage: Cinema Exposed' (2012)*

This second case study explores the curatorial strategy of 'Found Footage: Cinema Exposed', the inaugural exhibition of the EYE Film Institute Netherlands, in Amsterdam. In doing so, we enter the as yet unexplored grounds of cinema exhibitions; in other words, film curating in the museum. It is an addition to the overview of presenting film heritage given in section 6.2.

An exhibition room has traditionally white walls, the exhibited art works are conceived as a tangible 3D object set in a 3D space and the visitors are allowed to wander through this space at will. In contrast, a screening room traditionally has the form of a black box, where visitors are supposed to remain in their seat and watch projected images and added sound, set in a 2D frame. For a long time these two different areas were seperate domains, but the traditional distinction between cinema as 'Black Box' and the gallery as 'White Cube' has become blurred. The initiative of presenting crossovers started in the field of art accomodations. Artist films are increasingly shown as a part of modern art expositions in museums, galleries, art biennales and media art festivals. Erika Balsom (2013) thoroughly covers this area: she gives an overview of the research and discusses several examples of best practice of curating cinema and media art in galleries, such as the three temporary exhibitions held in Centre Pompidou in Paris in the 1980s and 1990s.

There are many more best practices of media art presentations to be noted, such as 'Notorious: Alfred Hitchcock and Contemporary Art' (Museum of Modern Art, Oxford, 1999), or 'Seeing Time' (San Francisco Museum of Modern Art, 1999), or 'Into the Light' (Whitney Museum of American Art, New York, 2001). Art historian Andrew Uroskie mentions *The Paradise Institute*, an installation made in 2001 by Janet Cardiff and George Bures Miller for the Canadian Pavilion at the Venice Biennale, as an examplary case study of a most direct artistic reflection upon the cinematic experience (2014: 1–5). More recently, the exhibition 'Erice-Kiarostami Correspondances' (2006) was presented in art galleries in Barcelona, Madrid and Paris, bringing together the Spanish director Victor Erice with the Iranian director Abbas Kiarostami in a retrospective and an installation, presenting their exchange of video letters (see Bergala 2006 and Ehrlich 2006). In 2006 the exhibition 'Beyond Cinema: the Art of Projection' was presented at Hamburger Bahnhof in Berlin. In 2012 an exhibition of expanded cinema was held at the Camden Arts Centre in London, aptly called 'Film in Space' and curated by British artist Guy Sherwin. For more examples of curating cinema in the setting of an art gallery or museum, see among others Wasson (2005), Nash (2006), Connolly (2009) and Uroskie (2014). Also artist photographers uses increasingly moving images in their projects. The exploration of cross-overs between cinema and photography offers an alluring perspective. Campany (2008) offers a thorough reflection on this.

The other way round, however, traffic of crossing borders is less dense. Modern media art, installations and artist films filter only slowly into the domain of cinema. For a long time the presence of experimental films in cinemas was restricted to incidental and marginal linear screenings for a small group of devotees. Recently there are some initiatives taken in the film festival circuit to establish more rapprochement between cinema and modern art. Evidence of this development is given by for instance the sidebar program 'Artist in Focus' of the International Film Festival Rotterdam. And media artist Mika Taamila curated in 2014 the theme programme 'Memories Can't Wait: Film Without Film', at the International Short Film Festival Oberhausen in Germany (see Balsom 2014). He is known for his mesmerising works, like the three channel video-installation *The Most Electrified Town in Finland* (2012), but he was also for many years programmer at Avanto, an experimental film festival based in Helsinki.

A curator at a film museum has a specific challenge to exhibit all aspects of cinema history. The traditional option is to choose for the option of a permanent exhibition of film-related objects, displayed in chronological order. Exhibits would usually consist of a line-up of traces of the distribution and exhibition of films (lobby cards, movie posters, cardboard cut-outs), combined with art work that give an impression of the production process, such as set photos, storyboards, skectches of costumes and sets, completed with all kinds of machinery and gear. The National Cinema Museum of Torino offers a best practice of this option (see Cere 2006). It is located in an impressive building, the Mole Antonelliana, originally conceived as a synagogue. The feature film *Dopo Mezzanotte* (*After Midnight*, Davide Ferrario, 2004) uses the exhibition as a stunning backdrop for its romantic story.

Another option for a curator at a film museum is to organise a series of temporary exhibitions. This option is used as a curatorial strategy by the EYE Film Institute Netherlands. It took a while before sufficient facilities were available to develop their ideas. In 2012 the institute moved to a new building in Amsterdam, where they finally could make use of a 1,200 square metre exhibition space, and a smaller permanent exhibition room in the Basement (see also the website eyefilm.nl). A unique feature of the approach of the EYE Film Institute Netherlands is that each exhibition is placed in context by an extensive programme at their screening rooms, with curatorial strands such as educational events (lectures, courses, workshops), cinema concerts (silent films with live music accompaniment), 'E-cinema' (experimental films), and 'Cinema Egzotik' (cult and camp, co-curated by Dutch film director Martin Koolhoven).

The exhibition rooms of EYE offer a totally new viewing experience, because the visitor is able to walk around projected images and choose their own itinerary. The traditional set-up of presenting film in a cinema hall is deconstructed by means of several loops on multi-screens. The essence of cinema '*dispositifs*' are explored and new options of presenting the wonder of film art are demonstrated. The exhibitions of EYE are examples of 'thinking outside the black box'; investigating the limits of the medium and crossing the borders between cinema, media art and live performances. Curator Jaap Guldemond can build upon a vast experience in curating exhibitions at major art museums. The opening exhibition at EYE can be seen as a retake on his earlier work for the international group exhibition 'Cinéma Cinéma – Contemporary Art and the Cinematic

Experience' at the Van Abbe Museum in Eindhoven (see Guldemond and Bloemheuvel 1999).

The exhibition 'Found Footage: Cinema Exposed' was held at EYE from 5 April to 3 June 2012, and was announced as follows:

> The exhibition and accompanying film programme reveals how artists and filmmakers utilize the virtually inexhaustible reservoir of images that can be found in film archives, on Internet, TV and DVD. This found footage serves as raw material with which they make new works and give new meaning to existing moving pictures. (Source: https://www.eyefilm.nl/en/news/found-footage-cinema-exposed-opening-exhibition-eye)

Some examples of works exhibited were: *Three Screen Ray* (Bruce Conner, 2006), a wild cut-up of ephemeral films; *Outerborough* (Bill Morrison, 2005), an artistic contemplation on a short 1899 travelogue filmed in New York; *Kristall* (Christian Girardet and Matthias Müller, 2006), a video installation mixing several mirror scenes taken from classic films; and *White Suits and Black Hats* (Arnout Mik, 2012) consisting of a compilation of colonial footage taken from the archive of EYE. Another commissioned work was *The Eternal Lesson (Replica)*, in which Christoph Girardet deconstructed an unfinished Dutch documentary about an art academy. In this way, the exhibition also made a clear connection to the archive collection of EYE and supported an awareness of the importance of preserving the film heritage. *Lyrical Nitrate* (Peter Delpeut, 1991) and other found footage films were screened as part of the sidebar programme of the exhibition. Director and former film curator Peter Delpeut contributed to the catalogue (see Delpeut 2012), his film is briefly discussed here below.

The reflective perspective of the opening exhibition was continued in subsequent exhibitions at the EYE Film Institute Netherlands, such as 'Expanded Cinema: Isaac Julien, Fiona Tan, Yang Fudong' (2012) and 'Cinema Remake: Art & Film' (2014). Another example of the curational strategy of reflection upon the status of cinema was the presentation in 2013 of a newly developed multiple screen installation made by Hungarian 'media archeologist' Péter Forgács: 'Looming Fire: Stories from the Netherlands East Indies (1900–1940)'. All his work as a director of found footage films has been acquired as part of the collection of EYE. The link

to the archive was therefore twofold: a contemporary artist who is prominently positioned in the collection was in 2013 commissioned to appropriate film heritage from the vaults of EYE. He selected images taken from
home movies made in colonial times in the Dutch East Indies and added
music and voice-overs reading fragments taken from historical private letters. Added together and put into space, this reworked heritage gave a
vivid impression of everyday life in the former colony. It also implicitly provided a reflection on representation, power structures and memory. More
information about the unique film style of guest curator Péter Forgács is to
be found in Bill Nichols and Michael Renov's volume (2011). Forgács was
introduced in the Netherlands typically by the gallery-based *World Wide
Video Festival* in the 1980s, and his films were first broadcast on Dutch
public television before they were screened at cinemas.

The exhibition space of EYE is also used to give immersive overviews of
works of special talents, such as Oskar Fischinger, Johan van der Keuken,
the Quay Brothers and the British artist Anthony McCall. During the summer
periods the line-up of EYE exhibitions are devoted to travelling exhibitions
and retrospectives of more generally well known directors, such as 'Stanley
Kubrick: The Exhibition' (2012), 'Fellini: The Exhibition' (2013) and 'David
Cronenberg: The Exhibition' (2014). This strategy also manifests itself in
many other film museums around Europe. A few examples taken from the
agenda of 2013 include the Martin Scorsese exhibition at the National
Cinema Museum of Torino, Jacques Demy in La Cinémathèque Française
in Paris, Satyajit Ray at the BFI Soutbank in London, Bernd Eichinger at
the Deutsche Kinemathek in Berlin, and Michelangelo Antonioni at the
Cinematek in Brussels. Around the same time the exhibition 'Pixar: 25
Years of Animation' travelled around the world, with stopovers in Paris,
Amsterdam, Hong Kong, Taipei and many other cities.

*Found footage: A first exploration*

Found footage films can be considered as a way of curating films: an idiosyncratic arrangement and editing of film heritage. We might refer to the
creator of found footage films or installations as a 'poetical curator'. The
artist creates something new by recycling available images and sounds.
This is in contrast to the editor of a compilation film who provides only
a series of film fragments mounted together in a reasoned way. In found

footage the artistic imagination is rooted in the personal way of processing archival stock, combining research and resources.

The domain of 'found footage' is a connecting term to indicate a set of very different artistic views on the re-use of all kinds of feature films and other film heritage. Professional filmmakers and artists can choose from a wide range of existing audio-visual material which is available in film archives or may be derived from private collections concealed in attics, basements or flea markets. In their work, they can react upon the whole spectrum of film heritage, which can be modified in diverse ways. Their palette consists of material from the period of early cinema (1895–1920), but also amateur films from all times, or educational films, corporate films and elements of the preliminary programme including cinema commercials, newsreels and trailers. The result is a growing number of very different examples of the 're-contextualisation' of historical images and sounds in the form of a new artistic work. For an overview see, among others, Wees (1993), Noordegraaf (2009), Anderson (2011) and Baron (2014).

The task of the film curator is therefore to find a conecting theme or angle in this growing stream of found footage. Here are some options to start with formulating a suitable programme concept. To some degree, found footage fits into the trend for nostalgia for earlier times. Movies can serve as a stimulus to the joy of recognising historical street scenes or landscapes, or more darkly, fuelling the melancholy at the sight of a lost era. Often an autobiographical element is recognisable in a found footage film, because its origin is usually a personal fascination. Some found footage films could be considered from the perspective of a fascination with historical images of faraway places and a redefintion of the 'exotic'. Every found footage film offers a inspirational tribute to the cinema productions of the past, in several different ways. Respect has many faces in this case, and there are various approaches possible. Labels such as 'spoof' or 'parody' imply comic imitation or magnification; 'pastiche' indicates that a film is composed almost entirely of borrowed fragments (see Dyer 2006). A special category of tributes are the fan-films and false trailers made by amateurs, and indeed the feature film *Be Kind Rewind* (Michel Gondry, 2008) is a playful handling of this phenomenon.

Found footage can be compared with similar approaches in other art disciplines, such as in the music industry ('sampling', 'remixing'), or in the field of graphic design ('collage', 'clip art', 'mash up'), visual arts (*'objet*

*trouvé'*, 'found art'), photography ('vernacular photography') and literature. A more recent label is that of 'self medias', with a choice of 'cut-ups'
and 'machinimas', short home-made video films derived from computer
graphics, especially taken from computer games.

'Appropriation' is another apt key word to indicate the re-use of existing film images in new art works. Found footage films process and rework
historical film material and re-uses it in a different context. The old moving
images are dusted off and this gives a new impetus to the presence of
forgotten films and neglected classics in the collective cultural memory.
In essence, found footage films provide a mediated connection between a
historical film culture and the current film experience.

*Lyrical Nitrate (Peter Delpeut, 1991)*

A good example of an imaginative approach of found footage is the film
*Lyrical Nitrate*. Its director, Peter Delpeut, worked as archivist, curator and
deputy director of the Dutch Film Museum between 1988–1995. He curated
an extensive programme on found footage films, among many others,
and he directed three found footage films himself, in which he presented
the archival treasures he had discovered. Besides *Lyrical Nitrate* he also
directed *The Forbidden Quest* (1992) and *Diva Dolorosa* (1999), and he
made the television programmes *Cinéma Perdu* (1995, also distributed
as videotape with an accompanying book publication). The whole team
of archivists of the Dutch Film Museum contributed to the on-going series
of compilations labeled 'Bits and Pieces' (see Olesen 2013). All this work
advocated the urgency of preserving the vulnerable film stock in the vault
of all archives, starting with the nitrate prints which were decaying fast.
For a vivid impression of the atmosphere in film archives in the 1990s see
among others Slide (1992), Surowiec (1996) and Smither and Surowiec
(2002). *Lyrical Nitrate* was the result of the preservation of a collection
of nitrate films coming from the heirs of Dutch distributor Jean Desmet. A
virtually complete catalogue of a distribution firm was saved just on time,
offering a unique insight into a historical film culture and the aesthetics
of early cinema; for more details see Blom (2003). In 2011 this collection
became part of the UNESCO Memory of the World Register and in 2014 it
was subject of a exhibition at EYE.

Peter Delpeut arranged the archival material in a thematic series, divided by intertitles such as 'Looking', 'Mise-en-scène', 'The Body', 'Passion', 'Dying' and 'Forgetting'.

> *Lyrical Nitrate* is a visual poem stringing together a variety of differ-
> ent clips from the material that Delpeut found. He doesn't attempt
> to construct a narrative so much as he composes a love song to
> early cinema. He arranges many of the snippets based on their
> relation to each other, finding recurring images and visual motifs
> to illustrate the tropes and styles that informed early moviemaking.
> (Rich 2008)

*Lyrical Nitrate* offers in many ways an explicit reflection on the essential characteristics of cinema: the presence of the camera, the expression of the actors, the composition of the frame, the manipulative capabilities of the editing, and the transience of the film material itself; see Delpeut (2012) and Habib (2008). Before the opening credits, attention is given to the often neglected issue of rendering a correct aspect ration in projec-tion; this is done simply by showing a square corresponding with the 1:1.33 ratio. The square contains a message to the audience: 'If you do not see the complete square, go to the operator and ask him to use the correct lens.' This notice is very helpful because presenting a film in the proper aspect ratio is too often neglected, most of the time out of sheer ignorance. A film curator should take care to respect the choices of the filmmakers, it is a fundamental responsibility.

Curating a screening of *Lyrical Nitrate* (50 minutes) offers a lot of options. The programme could start with the short *Liquidator* (Karel Doing, 2010, 8 minutes), based on the surviving decayed footage of an early Dutch city documentary, *Haarlem* (Willy Mullens, circa 1922). A next step could be the short film *Lyrical Data* (2012, 5 minutes) made by Belgian media artist Elias Heuninck. She demonstrated the fragility of the digital image by showing a distorted download of *Lyrical Nitrate*. With a total screening time of 63 minutes there is room for some relevant additional options. For instance the short film *Home Stories* (Matthias Müller, 1990, 6 minutes): a remix of scenes from Hollywood melodramas starring glamorous actresses as Grace Kelly, Tippi Hedren and Lana Turner, resulting in a reflection on stereotypes of representation and genre formulas. A total screening time of 69 minutes would be satisfactorily, but it is possible to consider to add the classic found footage film *Rose Hobart* (Joseph Cornell, 1936–39, 18 minutes) as finale. This remix of processed fragments of the Hollywood adventure film *East of Borneo* (1931) is made into an exceptional homage of actress Rose Hobart. In many reviews *Lyrical Nitrate* is compared with *Decasia* (Bill Morrison, 2009); see among others Cammaer (2009). It would be possible to schedule an interesting double bill, containing *Decasia* (70 minutes) side by side with *Lyrical Nitrate* and accompanying shorts. But it will be a challenge to attract an audience for this condensed linear screening. Alluring options are to add a Q&A or an inspiring introduction, possibly in combination with a workshop of composing found footage films, topped with a general competition for new talent. The confrontation with the logistic demands concerned will also be an appealing challenge.

*Conclusion*

The new curatorial strategy is to 'open up' the films, to place them into the three-dimensional space of an exhibition room, possibly in the context of relevant artwork and requisites. There are not many examples of this most innovative approach yet. EYE convincingly offers a view and a vision on potential possibilities. In this case study we could only offer a brief introduction of the curatorial strategy of EYE. It was not possible to discuss all their curatorial activities and film programmes. Further investigation and analysis is highly recommended. Also other best practices of exhibiting cinema are to be explored, worldwide.

# 8    CONCLUSION: FINAL WORDS

## 8.1 My Personal Version of a Justification of Film Art

In this short section I take up the challenge to formulate a convincing justi-fication of the importance and urgency of film art, shown in cinemas on the big screen. Cinema has a long history of emancipation and justification, but it is necessary to formulate this justification time and again, because cinema is positioning itself in a rapidly changing context. There are new possibilities in the choice of production tools which inspire filmmakers in different ways. There are also new developments in the infrastructure of distribution and exhibition. These different institutional circumstances will have consequences for the experience of film art. What is the beauty of cinema today? What is the relevance of it in our times?

Film art has always been a small subcategory in the domain of film culture. Formulated in marketing terms, film art is a niche market. Non-commercial film exhibition inevitably has a small market share. Giving attention to film art and caring about it requires, therefore, a solid defence. This challenge has only increased since the introduction of the Internet. Why should a consumer in the digital era spend time and money to watch a film in a screening room instead of watching it privately? And why should artistically excellent films be granted special attention? Is there a future for the quality cinema in the twenty-first century? Is it feasible for art cinema to remain a part of the repertoire of the exhibition circuit of the big screen? These are relevant questions, because the public visits art-house cinemas in relatively low numbers. Why is this regrettable? This brings us directly to the essence of an urgent justification of film art.

Before we can start to articulate an account of film art, it is necessary to examine once again a definition. The first option for this would be a search for the essential characteristics of film art. However, this option seems to be doomed, because the intrinsic value of film art is difficult to translate into a clear list of necessary and sufficient particulars. The inventory of required qualifications for a cinema artist does not form a solid base for a justification of film art either, because it is also very difficult to agree upon intersubjective criteria and design a reliable standard. There is no lack of nice labels, like 'authenticity', 'originality', 'spontaneity', 'sincerity', 'craftsmanship', 'involvement' and 'engagement' – but none of these are useful as unambiguous criteria. My strategy to get to a pragmatic definition of film art is to link the demarcation of film art to the activity of the viewer. I opt for a functional perspective, focusing on the effects of film art on the viewer. It is possible to separate this notion of activity of the viewer into three subcategories, following the distinctions of Michael Patrick Allen and Anne E. Lincoln (2004): the critical, professional and popular recognition of film art.

Film art is based on inspiration and imagination; film *circulation*, however, is largely based on laws of commercial value. Which films cinema spectators can see is determined to the utmost extent by people who are largely motivated by profit. The result is that film art has a low priority in their framework and that mediocrity is allowed, indeed promoted, if it makes money. Film art should be protected in this hostile environment of market operations through convincing justifications and celebrations.

In my view there is one clear dead-end street, namely searching for strictly economic arguments in the discourse of justification of film art. Granted, films do produce profits, because the visitors pay for their tickets and a lively cinema culture heightens in some way the attractiveness of the local business climate. This argument connects to the popular notion of the 'creative city', characterised by a high degree of dynamic innovation and social cohesion. This is indeed an alluring perspective, but these kinds of impact studies require a lot of calculations, which are most of the time debatable and also difficult to perform in a transparent way. It also narrows down the discussion of the value of film art to a restrictive accounting exercise of composing a balance of costs and benefits.

*Broadening horizons*

The best possible answer to the question of a justification of film art is, in my view, the qualitative argument that film art stimulates the cognitive activity of viewers. Film art in general enables the viewers to see the daily reality that surrounds them with fresh eyes. This positive disruption of habitual perceptions is known as 'alienation' or 'de-familiarisation', a translation of the German term *Verfremdungseffekt* developed by playwright Bertold Brecht in his epic theatre. The Russian formalists used the term *ostranenie* to denote this effect of art (see, among others, Thompson 1988 and Van den Oever 2009).

The core of my argument is the conviction that film art enlarges the diversity and variety of both the collective and the personal memory, and also enriches both shared and individual reference frames. Film art is an antidote to complacency and monotony; it increases the repertory of available narrations. It offers a wealth of possibilities for how to tell stories about one's position in the world, one's experiences in the past, view on history and imagination of possible futures. Film art nourishes the description and understanding of one's own identity: who am I; where do I come from? It gives inspiration to create various optional worlds, be they utopian ideals or dystopian nightmares. Film art enlarges the imagination of all kinds of possible worlds. As an example, the genre of 'fantasy films' comes in mind, but one might also think of films like *Drowning by Numbers* (Peter Greenaway, 1988) with its enlivening of boring reality by the inventing of complicated playing rules for an utterly useless game. In short, I am referring to film art as a qualitative positive impulse on the level of personal lives and societal discourse. This idealistic supposition about film art is surely debatable. Needless to say, it is very unsure which concrete, measurable positive effects film art could have on the behaviour and mental state of each member of the audience. Still, it is worthwhile and interesting to pose oneself the question: which films made a lasting impression on me, and why in particular? It is possible to do this firstly in retrospective, looking back on childhood and adolescence, and secondly looking around today, considering the films of this week or month.

Another approach would be to pose as many curious questions as possible and relate these to film art. For example: what did urban life look like in the Soviet Union in the 1920s? A film like *Tretya meshchanskaya* (*Bed and Sofa*, Abram Room, 1927) answers this question and gives a totally different and more subtle image than the stereotypes which haunt many history books. Another example: what does urban life look like in contemporary Iran? A film like *Chaharshanbe-soori* (*Fireworks Wednesday*, Asghar Farhadi, 2006) helps us to get an intimate view on this, arguably an even better one than you would get were you to travel to Tehran. And it isn't necessary to look for exotic locations or periods long ago to broaden one's horizons. Take for instance *El sol del Membrillo* (*The Quince Tree Sun*, Víctor Erice, 1992), a detailed observation of the Spanish painter Antonio López at work. He is trying to paint a tree in his sunny garden, more specifically a quince tree bearing yellow fruit. There is no plot; there is no action. Still, it is an outstanding example of film art, a fascinating reflection on how to observe the world, a demonstration of watching the sunlight in your backyard and trying to capture this. It is an example of 'slow cinema', a moment of rest in an otherwise restless series of distractions and sensations which dominate our contemporary visual culture.

## The diversity of film exhibition

My strategy for the composition of a definition and justification of film art is embedded in an institutional approach: film art could be described as everything that is accepted as film art by scientists, critics, film professionals and other authoritative experts. This perspective enables me to confront my own views on the relevance of film art and my personal aesthetic value judgements with the general discourse dealing with these matters. Following the institutional approach, the personal story of my viewing experience and my individualistic viewing history could also be framed in answer to the basic question: which films are accessible; which assortment of premieres, repertory films and film heritage is available? In my view, the supply of films should be as vast as possible, in order to offer a choice to a multiform audience. Diversity of film exhibition is key. The presentation of film art is possible in many ways, ranging from an exclusive screening in a big film festival venue to a solitary viewing on a laptop. These choices of facilities and infrastructure need to be cherished, because this diversity enables the spreading of film art. I advocate projecting films on a big screen, because there the circumstances are as they are supposed to be: a linear screening, a collective experience in a darkened room, watching the play of giant shadows with a concentrated gaze.

But is there a future for this kind of traditional film exhibition? Nowadays, film is available everywhere. Is there a need for public screenings in a cinema?

### 8.2 The Future of Cinema: Twenty-First-Century Prospects

If we want to look forward to the future possibilities of cinema curating, it is necessary to formulate an updated, personal answer to the fundamental ontological question: what is cinema?

In the deepest essence of its existence, cinema is an intangible product. The illusion of movement is the result of the combination of the 'phi phenomenon' and 'persistence of vision'. The correct projection of a strip of frames, or a stream of digital bits, causes the illusion of an apparently uninterrupted smooth movement. A series of time fragments seems to show time elapsing, thanks to a physical reflex of the human mind.

As a film curator it is possible to trace the choices of filmmakers working within the limitations of the basic essence of cinema. They can decide to depart from a mechanical registration of reality, or to create their own reality from scratch (the latter option is most clearly executed in animation films). The film camera functions more or less in the same way as a still camera, but it is a camera able to record 24 frames per second. To produce a live-action film means to first deconstruct the reality into a series of frame compositions, camera positions and camera movements. This raw material containing the mediated view of the camera eye is known as 'rushes'. The recordings are used to construct a new film reality by editing and sound mixing, adding effects and alterations. In many cases computer-generated images are added. Due to the digitisation of film production, the options to manipulate image and sound during post-production are increased, but this technological trend is just a minor detail. In essence a film consists of images and sounds that can only come to life in a continuous timeframe. The linear period of screening time is fixed, but within this framework filmmakers are free to jump back and forth in time and to mould it at will: they can stretch a moment in time indefinitely or, on the contrary, condense an action by fragmenting it. They can construct a coherent time and place, or create a chaotic world with a seemingly meaningless juxtaposition. Each choice is a neutral decision, neither wrong nor right. However, the way each option is handled by the film crew and cast is surely open to critical evaluation.

A film curator could apply a set of critical criteria to differentiate between excellence and mediocrity within the harvest of new films, or he could focus on film heritage and re-evaluate accepted classics or highlight unjustly ignored and underrated films. As Jared Rapfogel argues,

> film programming, at its best, helps start a conversation, putting different films in dialogue with each other and fostering an aware- ness of individual works as part of an oeuvre, a tradition, an historical era, or a nexus of relationships and interconnections – something that is easily lost when shopping among the hordes of films available on video or on-line. (2010: 38)

The prospects for cinema in the twenty-first century could be seen to be very uncertain. The popularity of cinema is being affected by the growing competition in the leisure market. The gross revenue in retail of computer games, for instance, became bigger than the revenue of cinema tickets several years ago. Is there a bright future for cinema? How long will there be an audience for new films? Is cinema becoming a fossil or a steady niche market? The celebration of the centennial of cinema in 1995 was a distinct moment of reflection on these questions. Besides many festive, celebratory programmes of revivals, there were also some predictions of 'The Death of Cinema', as noted in section 6.1. There are indeed a lot of empty cinemas worldwide. In each territory there are many local heritage projects consisting of mapping and sharing nostalgia about lost cinemas. There is also a variety of blogs about collective memories of shared pleas- ures in the cinema. Both the decay of cinema buildings and the remem- brance of past viewing experiences prompt many stories.

Once again, we live in a time of transition. The issue of the moment is the still recent move to digital distribution and exhibition and its conse- quences. Digitisation offers a lot of potential possibilities for 'speciality programming', such as cinema on demand, new forms of event cinema, and integration of alternative content (also called 'additional content'). But realising a wide variety of special film events still implies a lot of chal- lenging efforts. As a film curator in the twenty-first century, it is possible to choose to participate in the modification of existing institutional networks

119

or to explore possibilities for presenting aesthetic choices outside the existing structures of film festivals, film theatres and film archives. Some established examples of this alternative approach are respectively the 'CineFringe Festival' in Edinburgh, 'Secret Cinema' in London, and the 'Jack Stevenson Film Archive' in Denmark. Another option is using the concept of 'cinema on demand', or 'user-driven cinema exhibition', as discussed in section 4.2, based on critical mass ticketing channelled through online time-sharing user-groups and facilitated by online databases.

The roll-out of the digitisation of film exhibition and distribution has been well documented and analysed by several academic experts, including Harbord (2002), Willis (2005), Klinger (2006), Rodowick (2007), Tryon (2009), Bordwell (2012) and Tryon (2013). Future film historians will have ample documentation about the reception of this media change and the consequences of the 'digital turn'. For further discussion on the ontology of cinema in the twenty-first century, see among others Carroll (2008), Gaut (2010) and Isaacs (2013).

*Conclusion: Returning to the diversity of the cinema programme*

Not every film gets a worldwide release. Sometimes this is understandable, and sometimes it is unfair: the filmmakers miss an audience and the audience misses a relevant film. It is necessary for curators to attend to the flow of new films in their neighbourhood. If a curator's cinema is primarily an outlet for the big releases of international companies, then it certainly has an economic function, but the main purpose is limited to getting somebody else rich or at least remaining solvent. There is more to do for a film curator: to act as a dynamic force in the circulation of daring film releases and presentation of challenging film repertory. There is so much to investigate and to explore. A film curator needs to do a lot of research, watching films and reading about them. The overview of film history written by Mark Cousins (2004) for example offers offers an inspirational starting point for looking around with an open mind, searching with curiosity and enthusiasm for outstanding film productions, past and present. Curators create valuable memories by searching the supply of new films and digging into the available film heritage. A film curator has to check the international film festival circuit and discern the new harvest of notable films. The next step for a curator is to check their territory and see if these films get a release. If not, this provides a motivation to programme this as-yet-unknown film and attract an audience for these screenings. A film curator also has to check the content of the vaults of film archives – to circulate old films is to rescue them from oblivion. In both cases curators are defying the barriers of high costs, and in both cases they need a lot of cooperative professional friends.

Academic studies by UNESCO and other parties distinguish three formal aspects of cultural diversity: richness of variety; balance; and disparateness (see also Barclay 2011). Formulated in an operational way, achieving diversity of the programme in cinemas implies that curators develop a two-sided curatorial strategy. Besides offering new releases of high-graded international film productions, they have also to secure a variety of well-considered special event screenings, highlighting unreleased films of all sorts and a broad range of film heritage.

As mentioned in chapter two, there is the manifestation of a new cinephiliac conversation to be noted. The development of digital projection has emerged alongside an increase in options for audience interaction. In a quantitative sense this can happen through crowd-sourced film ratings on social media and IMDb, opinion aggregators and review search portals such as *Rotten Tomatoes*, as well as all sorts of web-based recommendation engines. In a qualitative sense there are new possibilities for expressing opinions in blogs and also creating dialogues, stimulating responses, producing crowd-sourced criticism and even sharing curating power. The overview of curatorial issues offered here is meant to stimulate this new conversation about cinema.

# BIBLIOGRAPHY

Acland, Charles R. (2003) *Screen Traffic: Movies, Multiplexes and Global Culture*. Durham, NC: Duke University Press.

Allen, Robert C. (1990) 'From Exhibition to Reception: Reflections on the Audience in Film History', *Screen*, 31, 4, 347–56.

\_\_\_\_ (2006) 'The Place of Space in Film Historiography', *TMG: Tijdschrift voor Mediageschiedenis*, 9, 2, 15–27.

\_\_\_\_\_ (2011) 'Reimagining the History of the Experience of Cinema in a Post-Moviegoing Age', in Richard Maltby, Daniel Biltereyst and Philippe Meers (eds) *Explorations in New Cinema History: Approaches and Case Studies*. Malden: John Wiley, 41–57.

Allen, Robert C. & Douglas Gomery (1985) *Film History: Theory and Practice*. New York: Knopf.

Allen, Michael Patrick and Anne E. Lincoln (2004) 'Critical Discourse and the Cultural Consecration of American Films', *Social Forces*, 82, 3, 871–94.

Altman, Rick (1999) *Film/Genre*. London: British Film Institute.

Anderson, Chris (2006) *The Long Tail: How Endless Choice is Creating Unlimited Demand*. London: Random House Business Books.

Anderson, Steve F. (2011) 'Found Footage', in *Technologies of History: Visual Media and the Eccentricity of the Past*. Lebanon, NH: Dartmouth College Press, 68–87.

Andrews, Dave (2013) *Theorizing Art Cinemas: Foreign, Cult, Avant-Garde, and Beyond*. Austin: University of Texas Press.

Arenas, Fernando Ramos (2012) 'Writing about a Common Love for Cinema: Discourses of Modern Cinephilia as a Trans-European Phenomenon', *Trespassing Journal*, 1, 18–33; http://trespassingjournal.com/Issue1/TPJ_l1_Arenas_Article.pdf

Aumont, Jacques ([1979] 1987) *Montage Eisenstein*, Bloomington, IN/ London: Indiana University Press/British Film Institute.

Austin, Thomas (2007) *Watching the World: Screen Documentary and Audiences*. Manchester: Manchester University Press.

Balcerzak, Scott and Jason Sperb (eds) (2009) *Cinephilia in the Age of Digital Reproduction: Film, Pleasure, and Digital Culture, vol. 1*. London: Wallflower Press.

____ (eds) (2012) *Cinephilia in the Age of Digital Reproduction: Film, Pleasure, and Digital Culture, vol. 2*. London: Wallflower Press.

Balsom, Erika (2013) *Exhibiting Cinema in Contemporary Art*. Amsterdam: Amsterdam University Press.

____ (2014) 'Live and Direct: Cinema as a Performing Art', *Art Forum*; http:// www.artforum.com/inprint/issue=201407&id=47842

Barclay, Alexander (2011) *The Cinema Industry, between Free Trade and Cultural Diversity: An Inquiry into Economic and Legal Aspects*. Saarbrücken: VDM Publishing.

Baron, Jamie (2014) *The Archive Effect: Found Footage and the Audiovisual Experience of History*. New York: Routledge.

Beardwell, Julie and Amanda Thompson (eds) (2014) *Human Resource Management: A Contemporary Approach*, seventh edition. Harlow: Pearson Education.

Becker, Howard (1982) *Art Worlds*. Berkeley, CA. University of California Press.

Behlil, Melis (2005) 'Ravenous Cinephiles: Cinephilia, Internet, and Online Film Communities', in Marijke De Valck and Malte Hagener (eds) *Cinephilia: Movies, Love and Memory*. Amsterdam: Amsterdam University Press, 111–24.

Belton, John (ed.) (2007) 'Film and Copyright', *Film History* special issue, 19, 1.

Bergala, Alain (2006) 'Erice-Kiarostami: The Pathways of Creation', *Rouge*, 9; www.rouge.com.au/9/erice_kiarostami.html;

Biltereyst, Daniel (2013) 'Cinema, Modernity and Audiences: Revisiting and Expanding the Debate', in Karina Aveyard and Albert Moran (eds) *Watching Films: New Perspectives on Movie-Going, Exhibition and Reception*. Bristol: Intellect, 17–32.

Blom, Ivo (2003) *Jean Desmet and the Early Dutch Film Trade*. Amsterdam: Amsterdam University Press.

Bordwell, David (1989) *Making Meaning: Inference and Rhetoric in the Interpretation of Cinema*. Cambridge, MA: Harvard University Press.

\_\_\_\_ (2008) *Poetics of Cinema*. New York: Routledge.

\_\_\_\_ (2012) *Pandora's Digital Box: Films, Files, and the Future of Movies*; http://www.davidbordwell.net/books/pandora.php

\_\_\_\_ (2014a) 'Observations on film Art: Zip, Zero, Zeitgeist'; http://www.davidbordwell.net/blog/2014/08/24/zip-zero-zeitgeist/

\_\_\_\_ (2014b) 'A Celestial Cinémathèque? or, Film Archives and Me: A Semi-Personal History'; http://www.davidbordwell.net/essays/celestial.php

Bordwell, David and Kristin Thompson (2013) *Film Art: An Introduction*. New York: McGraw-Hill.

Bosma, Peter (2009) 'The Bridge, seen in the perspective of the programme', *The Ivens Magazine*, 14/15, 44–7; http://ivens.nl/images/ivens_mag14.15.pdf

Boyle, Deirdre (2001) 'A Conversation with Péter Forgács', *Millenium Film Journal*, 37, 54–5.

Brownlow, Kevin (2004) *Napoleon: Abel Gance's Classic Film*. London: British Film Institute.

Buchsbaum, Jonathan and Elena Gorfinkel (2009) 'Dossier: Cinephilia. What is Being Fought for by Today's Cinephilia(s)?', *Framework*, 50, 1/2, 176–270.

Buckland, Warren (2000) 'The Semio Pragmatic Approach', in *The Cognitive Semiotics of Film*. Cambridge: University of Cambridge Press, 82–108.

Bywater, Tim and Thomas Sobchak (1989) *An Introduction to Film Criticism: Major Critical Approaches to Narrative Film*. New York: Macmillan.

Cammaer, G. J. (2009) 'Film Reviews: *Lyrical Nitrate*, directed by Peter Delpeut, The Netherlands 1990. *Decasia*, directed by Bill Morrison, USA 2002', *Convergence: The International Journal of Research into New Media Technologies*, 15, 3, 371–3.

Campany, David (2008) *Photography and Cinema*. London: Reaktion Books.

Carroll, Noël ([1979] 1996) 'Film History and Film Theory: An Outline for an Institutional Theory of Film', in *Theorizing the Moving Image*. Cambridge: Cambridge University Press, 375–91.

\_\_\_\_ (2003) 'Introducing Film Evaluation', in *Engaging the Moving Image*, New Haven, CT: Yale University Press, 147–64.

____ (2008) *The Philosophy of Motion Pictures*. Oxford: Blackwell.

Cashman, Stephen (2010) *Thinking Big: A Guide to Strategic Marketing Planning for Arts Organisations*. Cambridge: Arts Marketing Association.

Cere, Rinella (2006) 'Exhibiting cinema: the cultural activities of the Museo Nazionale del Cinema, 1958–1971', *Film History*, 18, 3, 295–305.

Chapman, James (2013) *Film and History: Theory and History*. Basingstoke: Palgrave Macmillan.

Cherchi Usai, Paolo (2000) *Silent Cinema: An introduction*. London: British Film Institute.

____ (2008) 'A Charter of Curatorial Values', in Paolo Cherchi Usai, David Francis, Alexander Horvath and Michael Loebenstein (eds) *Film Curatorship: Archives, Museums, and the Digital Marketplace*. Vienna: Austrian Film Museum/Syntagma, 146–60.

Cherchi Usai, Paolo, David Francis, Alexander Horvath and Michael Loebenstein (eds) (2008a) *Film Curatorship: Archives, Museums, and the Digital Marketplace*. Vienna: Austrian Film Museum/Syntagma.

____ (2008b) 'Case study #1: Curating the Documenta 12 Film Programme', in Paolo Cherchi Usai, David Francis, Alexander Horvath and Michael Loebenstein (eds) *Film Curatorship: Archives, Museums, and the Digital Marketplace*. Vienna: Austrian Film Museum/Syntagma, 130–40.

Cheshire, Godfrey (1998) 'The Death of Film/The Decay of Cinema', *New York Press*, 12, 34 (26 August); http://www.nypress.com/print.cfm?content_id=243

Colbert, François and Jacques Nantel (2012) *Marketing Culture and the Arts*. Montreal: HEC Montreal.

Cones, John W. (2002) *The Feature Film Distribution Deal: A Critical Analysis of the Single Most Important Film Industry Agreement and How the Motion Picture Industry Operates*. Carbondale, IN: Southern Illinois University Press.

Connolly, Maeve (2009) *The Place of Artists' Cinema: Space, Site and Screen*. London: Intellect.

Corrigan, Timothy (2006) *A Short Guide to Writing About Film*, sixth edition. New York: Longman.

Cousins, Mark (2004) *The Story of Film*. London: Pavilion Books.

Crofts, C. (2011) 'Cinema Distribution in the Age of Digital Projection', *Post Script*, 2, 82–98.

Decherney, Peter (2012) *Hollywood's Copyright Wars: From Edison to the Internet*. New York: Columbia University Press.

Delpeut, Peter (2012) 'An Unexpected Reception: *Lyrical Nitrate* between Film History and Art', in Jaap Guldemond, Marente Bloemheuvel and Giovanna Fossati (eds) *Found Footage: Cinema Exposed*. Amsterdam: Amsterdam University Press, 217–24.

De Valck, Marijke (2007) *Film Festivals: From European Geopolitics to Global Cinephilia*. Amsterdam: Amsterdam University Press.

____ (2010) 'Reflections on the Recent Cinephilia Debates', *Cinema Journal*, 49, 2, 132–9.

____ (2012) 'Finding Audiences for Films: Programming in Historical Perspective', in Jeffrey Ruoff (ed.) *Coming Soon to a Festival Near You: Programming Film Festivals*. St. Andrews: St. Andrew Film Studies, 25–40.

De Valck, Marijke and Malte Hagener (eds) (2005) *Cinephilia: Movies, Love and Memory*. Amsterdam: Amsterdam University Press.

Di Chiara, Francesco and Valentina Re (2011) 'Festival/Film History: The Impact of Film Festivals on Cinema Historiography. *Il cinema ritrovato* and Beyond', *Cinémas: revue d'études cinématographiques/Cinémas: Journal of Film Studies*, 21, 2–3, 131–51.

Di Foggia, Giacomo (2014) 'Cinephilia and Festivals: On the Need to Analyze the Lives and Ideas of Festival Founders' *Cinergie*, 6, 42–9; http://www.cinergie.it/?p=4929

Dyer, Richard (2006) *Pastiche*. London: Routledge.

Eakin, Emily (2011) 'Celluloid Hero: Tacita Dean's Exhilarating Homage to Film', *The New Yorker* (October 31); http://www.newyorker.com/magazine/2011/10/31/celluloid-hero

Ehrlich, Linda C. (2006) 'Letters to the World: Erice/Kiarostami: Correspondences Curated by Alain Bergala and Jordi Balló', *Senses of Cinema*, 41; http://sensesofcinema.com/2006/feature-articles/erice-kiarostami-correspondences/

Edmondson, Ray (2004) *Audiovisual Archiving Philosophy and Practice*. Paris: UNESCO; http://unesdoc.unesco.org/images/0013/001364/136477e.pdf

Elberse, Anita (2013) *Blockbusters: Hit-making, Risk-taking and the Big Business of Entertainment*. New York: Macmillan.

Elsaesser, Thomas, Alexander Horwath and Noel King (eds) (2004) *The*

*Last Great American Picture Show: New Hollywood Cinema in the 1970s*. Amsterdam: Amsterdam University Press.

Erickson, Steve (ed.) (2004) 'Permanent Ghosts: Cinephilia in the Age of the Internet and Video', *Senses of Cinema*, 4; www.sensesofcinema. com/contents/00/4

Fossati, Giovanna (2009) *From Grain to Pixel: The Archival Life of Film in Transition*. Amsterdam: Amsterdam University Press.

Frey, Mattias (2014) *The Permanent Crisis of Film Criticism: The Anxiety of Authority*. Amsterdam: Amsterdam University Press.

Frey, Mattias and Cecilia Sayad (eds) (2015) *Film Criticism in the Digital Age*. New Brunswick, NJ: Rutgers University Press.

Frick, Caroline (2011) *Saving Cinema: The Politics of Preservation*. New York: Oxford University Press.

Furby, Jacqueline and Karen Randell (eds) (2005) *Screen Methods: Comparative Readings in Film Studies*. London: Wallflower Press.

Gann, Jonathan (2012) *Behind the Screens: Programmers Reveal How Film Festivals Really Work*. Washington, D.C.: Reel Plan Press.

Gass, Lars Henrik (2009) 'Trade Market or Trademark? The Future of Film Festivals', *Rouge*, 13; http://www.rouge.com.au/13/trade.html

Gaudreault, André and Philippe Marion (2012) *The Kinematic Turn: Film in the Digital Era and its Ten Problems*. Montreal: Caboose.

Gaut, Berys (2010) *A Philosophy of Cinematic Art*. Cambridge: Cambridge University Press.

Gerstner, David A. and Janet Staiger (eds) (2013) *Authorship and Film*. New York: Routledge.

Gocsik, Kare, Richard Barsam and Dave Monahan (2013) *Writing About Movies*. New York: W. W. Norton.

Goldsmith, Leo (2013) 'Book review: *Found Footage: Cinema Exposed*', *Cineaste*, 38, 67–8.

Gomery, Douglas (1992) *Shared Pleasures: A History of Movie Presentation in the United States*. Madison, WS: University of Wisconsin Press.

Gorini, S. (2004) 'The Protection of Cinematographic Heritage in Europe', *Iris Plus: Legal Observations of the European Audio-Visual Observatory*, 8, 2–8.

Gorki, Maxim (1896) 'The Lumière Cinématograph', 4 July; http://www. seethink.com/stray_dir/kingdom_of_shadows.html

Grant, Barry Keith (2007) *Film Genre: From Iconography to Ideology*.

London: Wallflower Press.

Guldemond, Jaap, Marente Bloemheuvel and Giovanna Fossati (eds) (2012) *Found Footage: Cinema Exposed*. Amsterdam: Amsterdam University Press.

Guldemond, Jaap and Marente Bloemheuvel (eds) (1999) *Cinéma Cinéma: Contemporary Art and the Cinematic Experience*. Eindhoven/Rotterdam: Stedelijk Van Abbemuseum/ NAi Publishers.

Habib, André (2006) 'Ruin, Archive and the Time of Cinema: Peter Delpeut's *Lyrical Nitrate*', *SubStance*, 35, 10, 120–39.

Hagener, Malte and Marijke de Valck (2008) 'Cinephilia in Transition', in Jaap Kooijman, Patricia Pisters and Wanda Strauven (eds) *Mind the Screen: Media Concepts According to Thomas Elsaesser*. Amsterdam: Amsterdam University Press, 19–30.

Hagener, Malte (2007) *Moving Forward, Looking Back: The European Avant-garde and the Invention of Film Culture 1919–1939*. Amsterdam: Amsterdam University Press.

Hanich, Julian (2014) 'Watching a Film With Others: Towards a Theory of Collective Spectatorship', *Screen*, 55, 3, 338–59.

Harbord, Janet (2002) *Film Cultures*. London: Sage.

Herbert, Stephen (ed.) (1999) *A History of Pre-Cinema*. London: Routledge.

Hill, John and Pamela Church Gibson (eds) (2000) *Film Studies: Critical Approaches*. Oxford: Oxford University Press.

Hing-Yuk Wong, Cindy (2011) *Film Festivals: Culture, People and Power on the Global Screen*. New Brunswick, NJ: Rutgers University Press.

Hollows, Joanne and Mark Jancovich (1995) *Approaches to Popular Film*. Manchester: Manchester University Press.

Iordanova, Dina (2008) *Budding Channels of Peripheral Cinema: The Long Tail of Global Film Circulation*. San Francisco: Blurb.

____ (2009) 'The Film Festival Circuit', in Dina Iordanova and Ragan Rhyne (eds) *Film Festival Yearbook. Volume 1: The Festival Circuit*. St. Andrews: St. Andrews Film Studies, 23–9.

____ (2010) 'Mediating Diaspora: Film Festivals and Imagined Communities', in Dina Iordanova and Ruby Cheung (eds) *Film Festival Yearbook. Volume 2: Film Festivals and Imagined Communities*. St. Andrews: St. Andrews Film Studies, 12–44.

Iordanova, Dina and Stuart Cunningham (eds) (2012) *Digital Disruption:*

*Cinema Moves Online*. St. Andrews: St. Andrews Film Studies.

Iordanova, Dina and Ruby Cheung (2010) 'Introduction', in Dina Iordanova and Ruby Cheung (eds) *Film Festival Yearbook. Volume 2: Film Festivals and Imagined Communities*, St. Andrews: St. Andrews Film Studies, 1–11.

Isaacs, Bruce (2012) *The Orientation of Future Cinema: Technology, Aesthetics, Spectacle*. London: Bloomsbury.

Isenberg, Noah (n.d.) '*People on Sunday*: Young People Like Us'; http://www.criterion.com/current/posts/1904-people-on-sunday-young-people-like-us.

Jacobson, Roman (1960) 'Closing Statements: Linguistics and Poetics', in Thomas A. Sebeok (ed.) *Style in Language*. Cambridge, MA: MIT Press, 350–77.

Jankovich, Mark, Antonio Lazaro Reboll, Julian Stringer and Andy Willis (eds) (2003) *Defining Cult Movies: The Cultural Politics of Oppositional Taste*. Manchester: Manchester University Press.

Jeffers McDonald, Tamar (2007) *Romantic Comedy: Boy Meets Girl Meets Genre*. London: Wallflower Press.

Jovanovic, Stefan (2003) 'The Ending(s) of Cinema: Notes on the Recurrent Demise of the Seventh Art', part 1 & part 2, *Hors Champ*; www.horschamp.qc.ca/new_offscreen/death_cinema.html.

Jullier, Laurent and Jean-Marc Leveratto (2012) 'Cinephilia in the Digital Age', in Ian Christie (ed.) *Audiences: Defining and Researching Screen Entertainment Reception*. Amsterdam: Amsterdam University Press, 143–54.

Keathley, Christian (2006) *Cinephilia and History, or The Wind in the Trees*, Bloomington, IN: Indiana University Press.

Keen, Andrew (2007) *The Cult of the Amateur*. New York: Doubleday.

Klinger, Barbara (2001) 'The Contemporary Cinephile: Film Collecting in the Post-Video Era', in Melvyn Stokes and Richard Maltby (eds) *Hollywood Spectatorship: Changing Perceptions of Cinema Audiences*. London: British Film Institute, 132–51.

Klinger, Barbara (2006) *Beyond the Multiplex: Cinema, New Technologies and the Home*. Berkeley, CA: University of California Press.

_____ (2008) 'DVD and home film cultures', in James Bennett and Tom Brown (eds) *Film and Television After DVD*. London: Routledge.

Knight, Julia and Peter Thomas (2012) *Reaching Audiences: Distribution and Promotion of Alternative Moving Image*. Bristol: Intellect.

Koerber, Martin ([1998] 2000) 'Menschen am Sonntag: A Restoration and Documentation Case Study' in Mark-Paul Meyer and Paul Read (eds) *Restoration of Motion Picture Film*. Oxford: Butterworth-Heinemann, 231–41.

Kolker, Robert (2011) *A Cinema of Loneliness*, fourth edition. Oxford: Oxford University Press.

Kuhn, Annette (2002) *Dreaming of Fred and Ginger: Cinema and Cultural Memory*. New York: New York University Press.

Latour, Bruno (2005) *Reassembling the Social: An Introduction to Actor-Network-Theory*. Oxford: Oxford University Press.

Lobato, Ramon (2012) *Shadow Economies of Cinema: Mapping Informal Film Distribution*. London: British Film Institute.

Loiperdinger, Martin (ed.) (2011) *Early Cinema Today – KINtop1: The Art of Programming and Live Performance*. New Barnet: John Libbey.

Loist, Skadi and Marijke De Valck (eds) (2010) *Film Festivals/Film Festival Research: Thematic, Annotated Bibliography*; http://www.filmfestivalresearch.org/index.php/ffrn-bibliography

Lowenthal, David (1985) *The Past is a Foreign Country*. Cambridge: Cambridge University Press.

\_\_\_\_ (1998) *The Heritage Crusade and the Spoils of History*. Cambridge: Cambridge University Press.

Lury, Karen (2010) *The Child in Film: Tears, Fears and Fairy Tales*, London: I. B. Tauris.

Ma, Jean (2010) 'Tsai Ming-Liang's Haunted Movie Theater', in Rosalind Galt and Karl Schoonover (eds) *Global Art Cinema: New Theories and Histories*. Oxford: Oxford University Press, 334–50.

Macaulay, Scott (2012) 'How to Do a Festival Q&A', *Filmmaker Magazine*; http://filmmakermagazine.com/56822-how-to-do-a-festival-qa/#.UywbNlwYlXU

MacDonald, Scott (2002) *Cinema 16: Documents Toward a History of the Film Society*. Philadelphia: Temple University Press.

Marchessault, Janine and Susan Lord (eds) (2008) *Fluid Screens: Expanded Cinema*. Toronto: University of Toronto Press.

Marlow-Mann, Alex (ed.) (2013) *Film Festival Yearbook. Volume 5: Archival Film Festivals*. St. Andrews: St. Andrews Film Studies.

Martin, Adrian (2014) 'Combat Story', *De Filmkrant*, 362; http://www.

filmkrant.nl/world_wide_angle

Martin, Adrian and Jonathan Rosenbaum (eds) (2003) *Movie Mutations: The Changing Face of World Cinephilia*. London: British Film Institute.

Mayne, Judith (1993) *Cinema and Spectatorship*. London: Routledge.

Mercer, John and Martin Shingler (2004) *Melodrama: Genre, Style, Sensibility*. London: Wallflower Press.

Nash, Mark (2006) 'Questions of Practice', in Joseph N. Newland (ed.) (2006) *What Makes a Great Exhibition?* Philadelphia: Philadelphia Exhibitions Initiative, 142–53.

Nichols, Bill and Michael Renov (eds) (2011) *Cinema's Alchemist: The Films of Péter Forgács*. Minneapolis: University of Minnesota Press.

Nolan, Christopher (2014) 'Films of the Future Will Still Draw People to Theaters', *Wall Street Journal*, July 7.

Noordegraaf, Julia ([2008] 2009) 'Facing Forward with Found Footage: Displacing Colonial Footage in Documentaries and Video Art' in Liedeke Plate and Anneke Smelik (eds) *Technologies of Memory in the Arts*. Basingstoke: Palgrave, pp. 172–87.

Olesen, Christian (2013) 'Found Footage Photogénie: An interview with Elif Rongen-Kaynakçi and Mark-Paul Meyer', *Necsus*, 4; http://www.necsus-ejms.org/found-footage-photogenie-an-interview-with-elif-rongen-kaynakci-and-mark-paul-meyer/

Odin, Roger (2000) 'For a Semio-Pragmatics of Film', in Robert Stam and Toby Miller (eds) *Film and Theory: An Anthology*. Malden: Blackwell, 54–66.

Pariser, Eli (2011) *The Filter Bubble: What the Internet is Hiding From You*. London: Penguin.

Parks, Stacey (2012) *The Insider's Guide to Independent Film Distribution*. Oxford: Focal Press.

Parth, Kerstin, Oliver Hanlet and Thomas Ballhausen (eds) (2013) *Work/s in Progress: Digital Film Restoration Within Archives*. Vienna: Synema.

Pierce, David (2007) 'Forgotten Faces: Why Some of Our Cinema Heritage is Part of the Public Domain', *Film History*, 19, 2, 125–43.

____ (2013) *The Survival of American Silent Feature Films: 1912–1929*. Washington, D.C.: Library of Congress; http://www.loc.gov/today/pr/2013/files/2013silent_films_rpt.pdf

Pine, James H. and Joseph Gilmore (1999) *The Experience Economy*. Boston, MA: Harvard Business School Press.

Rapfogel, Jared (2010) 'Introduction to Repertory Film Programming: A Critical Symposium', *Cineaste*, 35, 2, 38.

Rastegar, Roya (2012) 'Difference, Aesthetics and the Curatorial Crisis of Film Festivals', *Screen*, 53, 3, 310–17.

Reis, J. (2011) *Think Outside the Boxoffice: the Ultimate Guide to Film Distribution and Marketing in the Digital Age*; http://www.thinkoutsidetheboxoffice.com

Rich, Jamie S. (2008) 'Review of *Lyrical Nitrate*', *DVD Talk*, March 2; http://www.dvdtalk.com/reviews/32524/lyrical-nitrate-forbidden-quest/

Rifkin, Jeremy (2000) *The Age of Access: The New Culture of Hypercapitalism Where All of Life is a Paid-for Experience*. New York: Tarcher/Putnam.

Rodowick, David N. (2007) *The Virtual Life of Film*. Cambridge, MA: Harvard University Press.

Rosenbaum, Jonathan (2013) 'Mark Cousins' Excellent Adventure: A Friendly and Innocent TV Odyssey Through Film History', *Film Comment*; http://filmcomment.com/article/mark-cousins-the-story-of-film-an-odyssey

Sallitt, Dan (2002) 'Sight Unchanged: How Did the Film Canon Get so Stodgy?', *Slate* August 20; www.slate.com/?id=2069759

Saunders, Mark M. K., Philip Lewis and Adrian Thornhill (2009) *Research Methods for Business Students*. Amsterdam: Pearson Education.

Schröder, Kim, Kirsten Drotner, Steve Kline, Catherine Murray (2003) *Researching Audiences: A Practical Guide to Methods in Media Audience Analysis*. London: Arnold.

Schulte-Strathaus, Stefanie (2004) 'Showing Different Films Differently: Cinema as a Result of Cinematic Thinking', *The Moving Image*, 4, 1, 1–16.

Scorsese, Martin and Michael Henry Wilson (1997) *A Personal Journey with Martin Scorsese through American Movies*. New York: Miramax/Hyperion.

Shary, Tim (2005) *Teen Movies: American Youth on Screen*. London: Wallflower Press.

Shoemaker, Pamela J. and Tim P. Vos (2009) *Gatekeeping Theory*. New York/London: Routledge.

Slide, Anthony (1992) *Nitrate Won't Wait: A History of Film Preservation in the United States*. Jefferson, NC: McFarland.

Smith, Caylin (2012) '"The Last Ray of the Dying Sun": Tacita Dean's commitment to analogue media as demonstrated through FLOH and

FILM', *Necsus: European Journal of Media Studies*; http://www.necsus-ejms.org/the-last-ray-of-the-dying-sun-tacita-deans-commitment-to-analogue-media-as-demonstrated-through-floh-and-film/

Smith, Laurajane (2006) *Uses of Heritage*. London: Routledge.

Smither, Roger and Catherine A. Surowiec (2002) *This Film is Dangerous. A Celebration of Nitrate Film*. Brussells: FIAF.

Sontag, Susan (1963) 'Against Interpretation', in *Against Interpretation and Other Essays*. New York: Farrar, Strauss & Giroux, 4–14.

\_\_\_\_ (1996) 'The Decay of Cinema', *The New York Times Magazine*, February 25, 60–1.

Stafford, Roy (2008) *Understanding Audiences and the Film Industry*. New York: Palgrave Macmillan.

Staiger, Janet (1985) 'The Politics of Film Canons', in *Cinema Journal*, 24, 3, 4–23.

\_\_\_\_ (2000) *Perverse Spectators: The Practices of Film Reception*. New York: New York University Press.

Staples, Terry (1997) *All Palls Together: The Story of Children's Cinema*. Edinburgh: Edinburgh University Press.

Strauven, Wanda (ed.) (2006) *Cinema of Attractions Reloaded*. Amsterdam: Amsterdam University Press.

Streible, Dan (forthcoming) *Orphan Films: Saving, Studying, and Screening Neglected Cinema*.

Surowiec, Catherine A. (ed.) (1996) *The Lumière Project: European Film Archives at the Crossroads*. Lisbon: Guide Artés Gráficas.

Tanner, Lauri Rose (2005) *Creating Film Festivals: Everything You Wanted to Know, But Didn't Know Who To Ask*; http://www.filmfestivalbook.com/FilmFestivalBook/TABLEofCONTENTS-CreatingFilmFestivalsBook.html

Telotte, J. P. (ed.) (1991) *The Cult Film Experience: Beyond All Reason*. Austin: University of Texas Press.

Thompson, Kristin (1988) 'A Neoformalist Approach to Film Analysis', in *Breaking the Glass Armor: Neoformalist Film Analysis*. Princeton, NJ: Princeton University Press, 1–46.

\_\_\_\_ (2008) *The Frodo Franchise: The Lord of the Rings and Modern Hollywood*. Berkeley, CA: University of California Press.

Totaro, Donato (2003) 'The "Sight & Sound" of Canons', *Off Screen*, 31 January; www.horschamp.qc.ca/new_offscreen/canon.html

\_\_\_\_ (2005) 'Susan Sontag: Against Interpretation?', *Off Screen*, 31

January; http://www.offscreen.com/index.php/phile/essays/against_
interpretation/

Tryon, Chuck (2009) *Reinventing Cinema: Movies in the Age of Media
Convergence*. New Brunswick, NJ: Rutgers University Press.

___ (2013) *On Demand Culture: Digital Delivery and the Future of Movies*.
New Brunswick, NJ: Rutgers University Press.

Tudor, Andrew (2005) 'The Rise and Fall of the Art (House) Movie', in David
Inglis and John Hughson (eds) *The Sociology of Art*. London: Palgrave
Macmillan, 125–38.

Turan, Kenneth (2002) *Sundance to Sarajevo: Film Festivals and the World
They Made*. Berkeley, CA: University of California Press.

Ulin, Jeffrey C. (2014) *The Business of Media Distribution: Monetizing Film,
TV, and Video Content in an Online World*, second edition. London:
Focal Press.

Uroskie, Andrew V. (2014) *Between the Black Box and the White Cube:
Expanded Cinema and Postwar Art*. Chicago: Chicago University Press.

Urricchio, William (1995) 'Archives and Absences', *Film History*, 3,
256–63.

Van den Oever, Annie (ed.) (2009) *Ostrannenie*. Amsterdam: Amsterdam
University Press.

Verhoeven, Deb (2013) 'What is Cinema? Death, Closure and the
Database', in Karina Aveyard and Albert Moran (eds) *Watching Films:
New Perspectives on Movie-Going, Exhibition and Reception*. Bristol:
Intellect, 33–51.

Waller, Gregory (ed.) (2002) *Moviegoing in America: A Sourcebook in the
History of Film Exhibition*. Oxford: Blackwell.

Wasson, Haidee (2005) *Museum Movies: The Museum of Modern Art and
the Birth of Art Cinema*. Berkeley, CA: University of California Press.

Wees, Wiliam C. (1993) *Recycled Images: The Art and Politics of Found
Footage Films*. New York: Anthology Film Archives.

Wells, Paul (2000) *The Horror Genre: From Beelzebub to Blair Witch*.
London: Wallflower Press.

Willis, Holly (2005) *New Digital Cinema: Reinventing the Moving Image*.
London: Wallflower Press.

Withall, Keith (2014) *Studying Early and Silent Cinema*. Leighton Buzzard:
Auteur.

Wojcik-Andrew, Ian (2000) *Children Films: History, Ideology, Pedagogy,*

*Theory.* London: Routledge.

Wollen, Peter (1993) 'Films: Why Do Some Survive and Others Disappear?', *Sight and Sound*, 3, 5, 26–8.

Youngblood, Gene (1970) *Expanded Cinema*; www.ubu.com/historical/ youngblood/expanded_cinema.pdf.

Zanichelli, Elena (2007) 'Interview with Alexander Horwath, Curator of *Gloria Kino*, the Filmprogramme of Documenta 12'; http://archiv. documenta12.de/index.php?id=1387&L=1

# INDEX

Milton Keynes UK
Ingram Content Group UK Ltd.
UKHW041039110224
437582UK00005B/372